Spirit Calls

The
Spirit Calls

*The autobiography of
internationally acclaimed
clairvoyant*

Peter Lee

ARROW BOOKS

Arrow Books Limited
62–65 Chandos Place, London WC2N 4NW

An imprint of Century Hutchinson Limited

London Melbourne Sydney Auckland
Johannesburg and agencies throughout
the world

First published 1986
© Peter Lee 1986
Written in collaboration with Christopher Hansard

Printed and bound in Great Britain by
Anchor Brendon Limited, Tiptree, Essex

ISBN 0 09 947820 X

*This book is lovingly dedicated
to my dearest mother and all those who
helped me along the hard road to understanding.
Peace to you all.*

Contents

Preface

By the Rt Hon. the Earl of Ypres

I am in some ways quite sceptical about the psychic world in general, but since my involvement with Peter Lee, I have found his predictions for me to be accurate, truthful and extremely helpful. I first met Peter through some friends of mine, and he was to them of considerable help and assistance in a time of great hardship and personal crisis. In many ways he helped, through his clairvoyance, to rebuild their lives back into a fine example of happiness and attainment.

I, like many people, I suppose, am mystified by such things as clairvoyance and its associated subjects but Peter dispels the mystery and apprehension. So when it comes to this subject I can only talk of my experience gained from one of the leading practitioners in the field, Peter Lee. Since I am a pragmatic man, I was amazed at how Peter was able to glean information from out of nowhere. So to you all that read this book, I can without hesitation say that you are in good hands and are bound, if I know Peter, to find yourself on a mysterious and entertaining adventure . . . the life of one of the world's greatest psychics.

Prologue

Looking back at my life, I find myself completely amazed at all that has happened to me, and all that has transpired in the world, over the last forty fast-moving years. There has been a total about turn in the way people live, and the world, since World War II, has changed for ever. I think of our ultimate future as a species full of divergent cultures and beliefs, and we are all in some way struggling to discover who, what and why we are.

And what of my own small role in the greater scheme of things? All those thousands of people – the famous and the infamous, the world-makers, the world-shakers, the rich and powerful, as well as the ordinary, honest hard-working individuals that I see every day – I think of how their lives have been helped or uplifted by consulting me. There is a greater force that has come from deep within me to guide and encourage others. Many times I have been unaware until a later date just how dramatically my predictions have changed people's lives. I see my role in society as an alternative to the psychologist, counsellor or even doctor, though I don't try to heal people's medical problems, unless I am prompted by Spirit.

Often I am a more relaxed version of the priest in the confessional, a modern-day wise man, if you like – a West End witch-doctor. Perhaps in previous lives I was a court jester who advised his ruler with clairvoyance, tomfoolery and satire, or a sorcerer-cum-advisor who gave omens of the future to his king. Many a time I have felt that I am a curious mixture of the two, and have wondered which is the wiser. But I portray the character which is relevant to the client. I don't put on airs; these qualities are just part of me. My skill is an art, created through an inborn gift which has been polished to exactitude by heartache and hard work.

My art is my existence; it is my creative contribution to making a better world. This ability, clairvoyance, lies dormant within everyone. Some people are more closely connected with it, by knowing *themselves*; if you know yourself, then you know everyone. Anyone can use it and everyone does, in times of great emotion and often without realizing it – and this has been the case since the time of our cavemen ancestors, when clairvoyance was their major tool of survival. The cavemen would use their clairvoyance to hunt down game, for their eyesight and hearing were poor. They knew where to go to find food, the best places to rest at night, and they were much in harmony with nature. If they were not so, they would die. Today the same holds true for us. Our ability of clairvoyance has withered away, by and large, through lack of use. But clairvoyance remains an essential part of the human make-up.

My own skill is used by a large cross-section of the local, national and international community. These days, all my clients come to me by that best possible form of advertising – personal recommendation. This brings me to a most important aspect of any psychic's work – the need for confidentiality and trust. No one, regardless who they are, wants their private information leaked to any Tom, Dick or Harry. From time to time in my book, I have mentioned certain names with the permission of those concerned. In the case of those who are deceased, I know without a doubt they would in no way be offended. How do I know? I've asked them! On the other hand, there are numerous people, famous, powerful, in the limelight and behind the scenes, who definitely do not want their names mentioned. How do I know? I've asked them, too.

There is within all our lives the invisible workings of karma – the energy of cause and effect. This energy is created by our actions, by our thoughts and our desires, and it affects both our inner emotional world and our place and success in the material world.

In the latter part of 1983, a client called Nina came to me for a reading. At that time Nina was beset by a tempestuous relationship, and she came to me to discover whether or not it would last. I said to her that by February 1984 this relationship would no longer be worthwhile. Naturally, she was upset, but then I told her that in December of 1984 she would meet the man with whom she would spend the rest of her life. Well, time passed, the subtle workings of cause and effect plied their course, and, in the middle of February 1985, Nina came to me once again with the same question – but this time it was about a different man! She came in and sat down, looking rather nervous.

'Peter, I've come back to see you because of the reading you gave me last year. Well, it all came absolutely true, just as you predicted, and now I've met another man, and I'm head over heels in love with him. I'm trying to fight it – I mean, I can't just fall in love with a man at first sight!' But she had.

I started my reading. 'This man, Nina, is coming through with a great deal of strength. I feel that he knows a great deal about the occult and psychic worlds, and has considerable talents as a psychic, but he has more talent as a writer. Is that right?'

'Yes, Peter, it is. He has come to England to become a writer.'

'Well, let me see, he is going to suffer a lot of heart-ache before he finds success. But he will eventually, and he will become a very successful writer. He will become famous. But I feel it will take time and, with you behind him, it will happen in a mature way. I feel, though, that at first he must start to write or be involved with what he knows a lot about. I feel he has studied psychology or something like that at university . . . But anyway he is the man for you. He will give you all that you want, and a great deal more.'

Well, at the time, little did I know that this young man, who had come all the way from New Zealand, would aid me in the writing of my book as my editorial collaborator. A few weeks after Nina had visited me, Christopher Hansard came to see me for a reading himself. In the reading I outlined how he would best gain success in the United Kingdom. At the time he was going through a phase that most serious artists endure, worrying about money, and wondering if they are being stupid in pursuing their art when they have little of anything but their own belief in themselves.

A few weeks passed. I was sitting going over some of the pages of my book – it was really a large bundle of notes at that time – when I felt a huge influx of psychic energy. The room grew very still, and like a dream, I was told by Spirit to contact this young writer, for he would help me with the book, and it would be a chance to launch his career. This energy from the spirit world told me that Christopher would be the one to adequately understand the message and meanings of a professional psychic. With his help I was able to whip this book into shape.

I hope that whoever reads my life story can learn from it. It may serve to spark a fire in some people, helping them to know that there is more to life than just daily routine. This book, however, is not just about me; it is a testament to the many thousands of men and women who have come to me for help and guidance. Their bravery and courage you will discover first-hand in the pages that follow. What use would I be without those who need my help?

I hope the day will come when everyone will be able to do as I and other psychics do – to read, see and interpret the very foundations of the human spirit. Then there will be greater self-awareness, and the problems shadowing mankind's future could be better resolved and potential catastrophe overcome.

This book is also about hope, wisdom, love and common sense – the most mysterious of all human qualities.

When I was a small boy, as fireballs lashed against the doors of our bomb shelter, breaking them down, I feared I was going to die – and in that moment I experienced a great sense of awe-inspiring peace. Now, writing this book has let me experience another profound peace – the peace of releasing the past and sharing it with my fellows.

What is it that makes me recall that experience so vividly? It is the spirit. The spirit within, the eternal spirit. The spirit calls – beckoning me on a new journey, a new adventure into life. Life is heaven or hell. Life is the only great adventure. Birth and death are resting-points along the way. How we live our life is the most important thing. No one can really apply any type of morality to the human spirit. If one must believe in something, believe in life itself. Although it changes constantly, its change is the only constant thing we have. All our experiences are nothing but extras on the side. Life is like a restaurant: you can order what you like for the main course, but the vegetables are an additional charge.

The spirit calls me on and ever forward. It creates a yearning inside me to know the reasons why we live. From within me, from the vortex of the spirit come my psychic gifts, but there is nothing supernatural about them. They are normal, part of our birthright – all we have to do is to realize that they are there.

The immense sparkling whirlpool of the moment is waiting to be experienced. It is safe – so won't you join me on my journey now, as we look back to the future? And you won't get hijacked as you take flight with me.

A word of thanks. Without the encouragement of my literary agent, Don Short, and my editorial collaborator, Christopher Hansard, this book would have never become a reality.

Peter Lee

Chapter 1
Dr Umaru Dikko

Reports in the world press and the accusations of the former military junta of Nigeria have sought in their time to discredit Umaru Dikko, one of Africa's most important political figures. Yet, perhaps sooner than people realize, this man will serve to unite his fractured homeland, Nigeria, and bring harmony back to a divided and strife-torn Africa.

Newspapers everywhere made a big story of Dr Umaru Dikko's kidnapping and his dramatic rescue by British security forces. Then the press went on to highlight a seemingly endless campaign by Nigeria to have Dr Dikko thrown out of Britain into the sweaty clutches of the Nigerian authorities. But how did these security forces know where to find the doctor? How did they know who was behind the kidnap plot? Well, I shall tell you. *I saved Dr Dikko's life.* It happened through a prediction I made. This prediction made it possible for those responsible for the plot to be arrested and tried. For when innocent people, like Dr Dikko, are at risk, then psychic forces always come to their aid!

To people who know Dr Dikko, it is obvious that the former junta embroiled him in trumped-up claims of fraud and embezzlement to make him the scapegoat for their own inept government. For towards the end of 1985, that very same government was ousted by a new regime. He was accused by that government of defrauding them of money intended to pay for a rice shipment and for other political uses. He was accused of stealing close to a billion pounds! But he never committed these crimes. I know, because my clairvoyance tells me so.

Their real grievance was that Dr Dikko had spoken out loudly and bravely against the oppression of his fellow countrymen by that military government. The whole Dikko affair, caused by their wish to have him extradited, became an issue of international human rights. If Dr Dikko had been forced to return to Lagos, only the worms within his grave would have gained any real benefit.

But now let me share with you the amazing truth of how my prediction was responsible for locating the doctor and saving his life. One day I was telephoned by a client, a prominent member of society who had being seeing me for some time. He seemed in acute distress and he asked me for a prompt reading. Because of his emotional state, I consented at once. My client, a European and a very trusted and respected friend of Dr Dikko's, soon turned up, out of breath and in a complete fluster.

That whole day up until then had had an uneasy feeling to it – an intense sense of foreboding. Perhaps subconsciously I had picked up the trouble already by psychic means. My cats, Trotsky and Chow-Chow, were on edge too, though once my client arrived they relaxed. Even the sky looked troubled and turbulent. After he arrived, it took a few minutes before he could speak calmly. He looked at me uncertainly, perhaps unsure if he should have come, but then suddenly he smiled, for he realized he had indeed come to the right person. Perhaps the only person who could help in this particular situation!

He took off his herring-bone coat, from a well-known

Savile Row tailor, and laid it down next to his trilby, scarf, and kid-leather gloves. Slowly he opened a box of Sullivan and Powell reserve blend, a truly exclusive brand of excellent cigarettes, then nervously said:

'Peter, have you heard about the kidnapping?'

'Kidnapping . . . whatever do you mean?'

'Dr Dikko, he's – he's being abducted! I'm really terribly concerned for his safety. I don't know what to do! That's why I've come to you. I know there isn't much time. Please help us find out what's going on, will you? Peter, please try. You're our only hope . . . !'

His pleading persuaded me to do my best, though my heart had almost stopped from all the surprise.

'Well, I haven't heard anything about this kidnapping, but let me tune in, and I'll see what I can do for you,' I replied, hoping for the best because I was extremely tired.

Special Branch had already been called in to help find the doctor, but for all their valiant and resourceful efforts, they had not come up with much. So my client had come to me for help, in the hope of passing on my impressions to the police and the other security services directly involved with the case.

As soon as I began to concentrate fully and tune in to the situation, I was inundated with huge amounts of electricity – a good sign that I was on the right path. Then in came copious amounts of random information. After sitting through it all, I finally started to get specific information that related to the case. For the moment, the doctor was clearly still alive.

The influx of information became ever stronger, until I reached the point where I entered the mind and senses of the unfortunate doctor . . . I felt as if someone had grabbed me from behind. People were passing by. Why didn't someone help me? I was thrown into a car, fighting and struggling! I then saw two African men in a violent struggle. I was involved in the fight and observing it at the same time. Then I was stunned. I felt the slow sticky trickle of warm blood. After that, I smelt congealing blood. A silence followed, accompanied by fear and the knowledge that I was trapped and could not escape! Then came muffled voices and the rhythm of a heart beating very, very slowly. Suddenly a sense of being struck – a cramping pain! Next came rough, callous handling; I was pushed into a corner and kicked. Men were talking somewhere in quick, arguing tones. It seemed something had gone wrong, something had been botched. Faintly I heard the mention of a Nigerian Airways plane. Then I was pulled to my feet and again thrown into the back seat of a car, and it drove off very fast. I felt drugs of some sort being injected into me. Rubber tubes were shoved into me. Manacles were clamped on to my hands and feet. I felt sick. An overwhelming sense of depression and coldness washed over me. My head was spinning. The world seemed far away, and very threatening. I was alone. Then came a heaviness, an almost unbearable heaviness, and finally – in a flickering vision that must have been the doctor's last sight before he collapsed – I saw a terraced house with a number on the gate. Everything went black.

There came the sound of another car pulling up. Some African language was spoken. A car door slammed and I heard the roar of a jet aeroplane above me, and the smell of its fumes. Even though I had tuned in to the doctor's almost unconscious state, I knew that he was very close to an outer London airport. For at least twenty minutes I picked up nothing but the doctor sinking into an ever deeper state of enforced unconsciousness. Then the drugs started to wear off

– but quickly more were administered. Nothing else happened for a long time. There were gags biting deep into the corners of my mouth and my gums, making them bleed. Slowly the doctor was waking, but of course he could not speak. He could not even make a sound. The drugs seemed to have paralysed him in some way. I felt as if I was waking from a terrible nothingness. I then realized I was enclosed in a crate or large box. The smell of treated wood was suffocating. An almost hysterical sense of claustrophobia engulfed me.

At that moment I had to stop the reading; I needed to rest. A sudden gut feeling – the doctor was in mortal danger! I could sense the threat of death. There would be no tin-pot trial for him. He might never even arrive in Nigeria, but mysteriously disappear on the journey.

I also began to pick up impressions of the van or car into which he had been bundled. Things started to go in reverse order. It only meant one thing: that Dr Dikko was near death, badly overdosed.

As I concentrated, I sensed that African and Middle Eastern people were involved. But I had to get back into the present moment. I concentrated even harder, and slowly more precise information began to come to me. I began to home in on an airport . . . where was it? It came back to me – on the outskirts of London. But what was the name? Slowly letters began to form in front of me, the first letter was S, then came a T, an A, then nothing, finally a D. I concentrated further. It came – this airport on the outskirts had to be Stansted. I knew he would be found there!

I began to inform my client, but then more information came. I heard a voice, and saw in my mind's eye a clock – a twenty-four hour clock. The hands were pointing to the number twenty-four. Suddenly the clock cracked. It began to bleed symbolically, and as it turned into a tortured face, a beautiful, resonant voice spoke to me, '*Twenty-four hours only! Twenty-four hours only or he shall die!*'

I then knew this was a real message from a higher force, and immediately told my client all that had happened. He was incredibly thankful for this revelation, and gathering up his coat and gloves went off as fast as he could to inform Scotland Yard.

After he departed, I began to direct large amounts of psychic energy into Stansted Airport, in the hope of helping obstruct the kidnappers' plot to remove the doctor from the United Kingdom. I first concentrated on the Nigerian Airways airliner, thinking of obstruction by Customs and problems in loading. The higher forces were with me that day, because I am sure that what I did actually did help thwart the criminals.

Meanwhile, with precision and direct action, the police intercepted the kidnappers at Stansted Airport.

A few days later, my client returned, beaming happily. He assured me that everything took place as I had predicted! The authorities had found Dr Dikko in a packing case, bound like an animal, drugged to the eyeballs. The crate he was held in was labelled *Diplomatic Cargo* in bright red ink. A Nigerian Airways cargo plane normally consigned to carry forty tons was standing ready for take-off, with a load of only four and a half! After I listened to my client's report, we celebrated with a drink, toasting first the doctor's safety. Then I told my client how I had sent out disruptive energy to hamper the kidnappers from shifting their cargo. After listening intently, my friend disclosed what had taken place almost exactly at the time when I was sending out this energy. An extremely dutiful Customs officer, Mr Charles Morrow, became highly suspicious about why the Nigerian Boeing 707 should be kept

22

overnight at Stansted Airport without any proper reason, so he went to investigate. In the cargo bay he discovered two crates being unloaded rather quickly on to fork-lift trucks, surrounded by a large group of Nigerians. Mr Morrow began to ask questions. Then a Nigerian diplomat produced the now infamous baggage labels marked *Diplomatic Cargo*. Mr Morrow felt impelled to approach the crates, but the pilot, Yusufu, confronted him and insisted that the crates should remain closed. Obviously intent on doing his duty, Mr Morrow warned the Nigerian that he would be arrested if he continued behaving in an obstructive and threatening manner.

The psychic energy that I was directing was starting to do its work. I seldom use this – and only in extreme cases like this, when justice has to triumph. People intent on murdering an innocent man should never be allowed to get the upper hand. And it seemed that the natural justice of the universe acted far more swiftly than even I thought it would, even with a little help from me.

There was then a slight flurry of angry words and insults from the Nigerian contingent. Mr Morrow left the cargo bay full of suspicion. Later that evening, Essex Police officers arrived and, without further argument, the crates were ripped open. What they found there shocked them deeply. They saw Dr Dikko huddled up, with an astonished accomplice to crime, Dr Shapiro, by his feet. Dr Dikko was very, very unconscious. Attached to his body was an electro-cardiogram to monitor his fragile heartbeat, while intravenous drips had been inserted into his arms without any real care. Near the prone doctor were an oxygen cylinder and a mask.

The victim had started to vomit, so Dr Shapiro, an

Israeli anaesthetist, had shoved a plastic tube down his throat to clear his air passage. Dr Dikko had been pushed into a crate only four feet by four feet. No wonder I had sensed the stifling agony of claustrophobia!

The police quickly seized the ringleader, Alexander Barak, and his sidekick, Felix Abitbol. The trouble-making 'pilot' – as he was dressed when apprehended – turned out also to be a Nigerian diplomat. Mohammed Yusufu claimed that he had no idea what was in the crates, and was merely ordered to take them to Lagos. It came out in court that Yusufu had taken five hundred pounds from the Nigerian High Commission safe to buy these crates, and they had apparently been specially built with airholes by a joinery company in a London suburb. In court it came out that when he arrived out at Stansted, he was shown Dr Dikko already in a state of deep unconsciousness. The Israeli doctor, Shapiro, said Barak told him that kidnapping Dr Dikko would ultimately be of great benefit to Israel. Obviously he was a very impressionable man. Dr Shapiro was paid the sum of two thousand pounds four weeks before the Dikko affair to purchase all the drugs and medical equipment he would need. The ringleader, Alexander Barak, was no more than a bounty-hunter. He claimed that a group of businessmen had approached him to capture Dr Dikko alive. Tests made on Dr Dikko revealed that his kidnappers had dosed him with near-lethal amounts of a drug called Pentothal. Pentothal is widely known as a 'truth drug', and often used as an anaesthetic.

Dr Dikko was able to make a healthy recovery at the Herts and Essex Hospital at Bishop's Stortford.

*

Since his terrible ordeal, Dr Dikko has come to me for consultations, as have also members of his staff and friends, and I have also had the pleasure of going to his home. Psychically, I have found his character to be honest and impeccable.

I mentioned to Dr Dikko in one of our many consultations that he would face a few more ordeals, but none as severe as the kidnap attempt. However, with his common sense, his strong awareness of destiny, and his application of intelligence, he would come through all the ordeals that came his way.

From a deep love for his own country and its great natural beauty, Dr Dikko much wanted to return one day to Nigeria. I made a prediction for him which raised two major points. I told him of how the then military junta would fall like leaves in winter due to its own stupidity and the in-fighting among its members. Then, perhaps, a more relaxed regime, friendly to Dr Dikko, would consult him in some way. But, without warning, there would be a revolution in Nigeria and eventually true civilian government would be returned to power – and this would include Dr Dikko himself. He would end up in a far stronger and more influential position, enabling him to do more good for the ordinary people of that foodbowl of Africa. *I know from my psychic observations that Dr Dikko will return from the wilderness, his name totally cleared.*

I also had to tell the doctor that he would be in for a major disappointment concerning his request for political asylum. But being denied asylum would not mean that he would be removed from the United Kingdom. Psychically I was sure that the British government would in no way entertain the extradition request made by the spiteful Nigerian government of the time. I told him not to worry, and in time this prediction came true. However, it was a long and tiring battle for him.

The kidnappers received stiff penalties for their crime, classified as terrorism. Alexander Barak received a fourteen-year jail sentence. Mohammed Yusufu went down for a twelve-year term. Dr Shapiro, who seems to have been tricked into the whole plan and had become the fall-guy of the bungled operation, was given a ten-year term, as was the other conspirator, Felix Abitbol.

In one of Dr Dikko's readings with me, the spirit predicted in very certain terms that Dr Dikko would go to the Caribbean. There he would be hailed as a hero of political change. From there, he would eventually return to Nigeria, in well-earned triumph. On his return he would have the complete support of the nation. But with regard to the revolution I predicted, I felt that there would be comparatively little bloodshed, and there would be a great deal of help offered to him by a French-speaking country. Britain also seemed to play a role in the liberation of Nigeria, through peaceful means.

The greatest danger to Dr Dikko still comes, I feel, from America. Whether this be from the government there, or some other group, or a New York-based individual, I was not sure. But what I did know was that the doctor should steer well clear of the United States.

Umaru Dikko is not a tall man. He projects vitality and charisma born out of challenge and survival. He is an aristocrat by birth, and this is evident in the way he conducts himself. He does not smoke, drink or take drugs. He is a devout Moslem but extremely tolerant, a man who loves peace and harmony. Softly spoken, well mannered, he emanates a feeling of deep peace and contentment. I know this because of my psychic insight. Such peace would not be within a man if he had defrauded the poor of Nigeria by stealing money needed for food and essential services of government.

My psychic impressions about Dr Dikko and his mission are correct, and history will prove them to be so. Dr Dikko is born to be the leader who will transform Nigeria. All Africa will benefit because of this. He will lift Nigeria's economy and make it happy and prosperous once more.

Dr Dikko knows that when he needs me, I will be ready to help him as an oracle for truth, a shaman for sanity. For he realizes that there are more mysteries under heaven and earth than are at first apparent.

Chapter 2
Almost Like Forever

The shelter shuddered and groaned under the impact
of the bombs. Outside, ugly red flashes of light filled
the sky. It was as if the clouds were bleeding to death
and I could hear their cries. The window I peered
through was suddenly covered in ash and grime. The
shutters that once covered it now lay broken in pieces
on the ground. I heard people yell. Voices were coming
closer. I saw aeroplanes coming. Then there was
silence. Strange. Threatening. London was holding its
breath. Then people began to yell and scream. The
voices came closer.

'Hey! Look out . . . Quick! For God's sake get out
of the way – there's one right behind you!' A deafening
boom ripped through the air, hurling open the doors to
the bomb shelter. Dust, smoke and a strange burning
smell filled the room. The air filled with thin, high
whistles – whistles of death. The bombs were falling.
All I could see was a swirling mucky red, and the
outlines of people, like ghosts on the edge of hell,
running back and forth, terrified.

It was as if hell had come to earth. Without warning,
the candle in the shelter went out. I was left in brooding
darkness. For the first time in my young life, I felt
alone. Scared. Vulnerable. I started to cry. Where was
my mother? Then in the distance I heard her voice,
calling, calling – then footsteps. Once again the screeching of bombs filled the air.

The footsteps broke into a mad run.

'Mummy!' I cried. 'Mummy, where are you?'

A dim figure entered the shelter, out of breath. There was the sound of a striking match and the security of the candlelight spread through the shelter, making the dusty air glow. My mother's arms encircled me, keeping me safe from harm. This was my earliest childhood memory.

I was two years old at the time. Being born into war-ravaged London served to heighten the development of my psychic abilities. At that young age, war woke me up to life. The carnage and destruction hit home. I have always therefore known the closeness that develops among people in such times, closeness born out of fear of death and the desire for survival.

My parents had a bomb shelter in their back yard, which they gladly shared with friends and neighbours. I was always surrounded by happy people, eager to help each other out if anyone was really short of provisions.

I sincerely hope that such times never come again, for there may be no second chance this time. Food and clothing were of course in short supply, but then there was always music to make everyone smile. The London Shelter Orchestra, it was jokingly called. In my parents' shelter everyone who could play or sing was an automatic member. 'Come on, Bill, play your ukelele and make the baby laugh.' Naturally people always tried to make me smile, an infant with a serious face – the young Peter Chambers. Everyone would laugh when I did – such is the power of a baby. In the fraternity of the bomb shelter, life seemed to me to be one big party – even though the war was just a few feet away from the doors.

I was born into this world on 18 September 1940, under the finicking sign of Virgo, at St Alban's Road,

Highgate. Soon afterwards – the shock of my arrival probably being too much for the neighbours (apparently my crying was louder than Caruso's best night) – my family moved to Malden Place, in Kentish Town. This was the house I later called 'the bomb-shelter house'. Malden Place was a beautiful house: it had space and a very homely atmosphere, created by my mother's peace of mind.

One of the most dramatic events of my early life occurred when I was walking through the ruined and desolate suburb of Gospel Oak, not far from where I lived. I saw a sparkling, gleaming object amongst the rubble. It was the prettiest piece of metal I had ever seen. As I picked it up I began to feel giddy, slightly disorientated, and for a moment I blacked out. As I came to I had the sensation of flying high in the sky and, looking down, I could see Gospel Oak intact. Something was wrong; how could it be that so many of the buildings were still there? Suddenly I was falling, plummeting to the ground, the air hissing past me. There was a great roar. Flames everywhere. Then that strange burning smell again. I did not understand what was happening.

I was on earth again. There was no raging fire anywhere – all around was grey rubble and the flattened remains of shops, houses, cars. The very air was dusty, and a few small fires dotted the landscape. The wind was cold. A lonely-looking dog limped across the road. Somewhere a siren started up like some perverse hymn to the waste around me.

When I got home and showed my mother this pretty piece of metal, she almost jumped out of her skin. She recognized it immediately for what it was – part of a tail-fin from a flying bomb – doodlebugs, they were called. I was given a spanking for wandering so far from home, and I was told never to touch things like that again. But I did!

My mother threw it away in the rubbish bin, but I searched until I found it. For me this was the key to a mystery – an entrancing magical jewel that answered a deep unspoken need within me.

Looking back on that experience, I now know that it was my first experience of psychometry. Psychometry is a type of divination where the psychic can discover events of the past, present and future by tuning in to the vibrations that emanate from objects. Gradually I realized that I had some kind of very special ability. This was unique to me, I assumed, and I wanted to know more . . .

I hid the tail-fin in a secret place, and there, by tuning in to it, I began to see the faces of strange men in uniforms and places far away. I saw events before they actually happened. It was exciting and frightening, but it all seemed part of me.

There is a curious mixture of blood in my veins which may have helped to give me my psychic abilities. My mother's family originally came from Ireland but settled in South Wales. Her family never saw Ireland again. They were all fervent Roman Catholics, and my mother's father, strong, stubborn and self-willed, was one of Baden-Powell's most important aides. He saw many combat situations at the great man's side, and was instrumental in helping that great soldier secure the relief of Mafeking.

My mother inherited some of her father's qualities, but with her strength and iron will she also combined a highly developed sense of compassion. She was a deeply religious woman, but was never in any way a Bible-basher or fanatic. She was the eldest of three daughters and, through need, had a very capable air about her.

For many years, heirlooms of Baden-Powell's were passed down through my family, and I would take any chance I could get to spend time on these objects, developing my psychometry. My favourite was Baden-Powell's floating knife. From it I picked up Baden-Powell's private thoughts; and I saw glimpses of the conflict in the Boer War.

My father's family came from Dover, not far from the famous White Cliffs. They were of hard-working, down-to-earth stock. To my father, life was either black or white: there were no grey areas. Nothing could be left undefined. My father was an aviation engineer, and he built planes in those wild and daring days when they were still made out of wood, brown paper and string. But as technology advanced in leaps and bounds, and the brooding threat of war rumbled on the shores of Europe, he began to use his expertise on cars, heavy goods vehicles and other kinds of wheel-based vehicles.

My father was an absolute wizard with all types of machinery, and around the home he could fix or invent anything that was ever needed. He was not a religious man in any way, but he was a devout atheist – a religion of sorts. At times, this caused friction between my parents, but they always managed to respect each other, in an all-embracing way that blended humour, compromise and a deep but restrained love for each other. My father did not reveal his love for my mother in any very obvious way, but it was there all the same.

He firmly adhered to the tenets of socialism and the entire labour movement. It was the plan for perfection on earth, as far as he was concerned. He opposed the Establishment with a vengeance, and advocated to the world, his family and his few close friends the sparkling wonders of the Welfare State till his dying day. In his eyes, wearied by the grim reality of never having enough to make ends meet, socialism could do no wrong.

I feel that this attitude was primarily due to the somewhat cruel circumstances in which his own father died, to whom he was very close. During the war, my father went through a very bad financial period. When his father fell seriously ill, mine called for an ambulance – but it arrived one whole hour after grandfather died. My father was, of course, heartbroken – and yet he was still made to pay for the ambulance. He blamed 'the system' for his father's death, and carried this grief silently, and in tremendous emotional pain, all his life.

In many ways my father was an insensitive man. I'm sure he never really realized the consequences for those who loved and cared for him. One example, which stayed in my mother's mind all her life, was that on the day they were to choose their engagement ring, he decided not to go, and sent his own mother along in his place!

My father's mother was a most interesting woman. She had a great deal of natural wisdom and foresight, and an extremely strong natural clairvoyance which was often highly accurate. My mother and she were very good friends and respected each other for their sense of values and pride in their homes, and not just because my mother was married to her son. My last meeting with my grandmother was to change my life totally and for ever, and in the end it would create for me my special place in the universe.

I had three sisters and a brother. Mary and Eileen were older than me, and Pauline was younger. Bernard was a few years older. There was quite an age gap between me and the first three, so I never really got to know them that well, but with Pauline I had a friendly relationship. At my mother's death, a special bond formed between the two of us. As a child, though, I spent a lot of time by myself, exploring the psychic mysteries that so intrigued me. I found, for instance, that I could see the auras around people, animals, plants and objects. The aura is the force-field of energy surrounding us that is like an emanation from our mental and physical energies.

As for school, from five to thirteen I attended St Dominic's Priory in Hampstead, which was a very friendly place and ideal for young children; the staff were truly dedicated to their work. Later, after a brief but diabolical encounter with another Catholic school made up of priests who did not care much for their jobs as teachers, I went to a technical school until I was eighteen. In many ways my early childhood was like any other boy's, and I did not quite realize how different I was from other children for quite some time.

Often my special gifts would seem to operate of their own accord, and I began to know things about people – their deep, dark, embarrassing secrets, things that little boys should not know. That Mrs Jones was 'having it off' with the local motor-mechanic, or that Mr Smith was deliberately quiet about his shady past. Things like that popped readily into my head through my clairvoyance, and innocently I would ask these people about their private affairs. Long embarrassed silences would follow, then comments like, 'So you spy on other people, do you? What a rude little boy!'

When my mother, Christina Mary Anne Driscoll, said yes, and married my father, Albert Edward Chambers, little did she realize what a little bundle of trouble I was going to be! At one point in my 'career of naughtiness', as my grandmother called it, I used to go around with a mischievous but relatively innocent street gang.

Often we would declare war on the boys in the next street, with victories and losses coming out fifty-fifty. London in those days was a garbage heap, a huge pile of rubble created through war and through demolition to make way for new buildings. All of us would play at soldiers, which seemed quite natural then, as there were plenty still hanging about, uneasy and unsure of their purpose. My involvement with the street gang was cut short when my best friend and I, after some silly antics with a low-powered airgun, took practice shots at the rear end of a rather fat boy, the local Billy Bunter. His father turned out to be even larger in proportions – and also a policeman! He grabbed us both by the scruff of the neck, took us home and let natural law take its course. From that day on I stayed home a lot, and for a few days found it rather difficult to sit down for any length of time . . .

But through this, I discovered an inner world, one of fantasy related to my psychic skills, and so quite naturally I began to explore them. I began to see people in spirit, and the two nice little old ladies who lived down the road would often pop in to say hello and gossip awhile as they did when they were still alive. I do not think that the fact of their death had quite dawned on them. After I had seen lots of these 'people', my mother became extremely worried, and took me to the doctor. He was a wise old man, and a spiritualist, and suggested to my mother, in stern but polite terms, that she should perhaps try to believe me. My poor mother was taken aback. Her little boy was seeing ghosts! What next?

By trial and error I learnt how to control, direct and refine my psychic skills. I would spend time concentrating on objects to develop my psychometry, and I would also try to predict minor events before they happened – like who would be speaking at the other end when the phone started ringing.

But eventually I reached an age when I wanted to *belong* to a group once again, so I joined the Boy Scouts. I went off on one of their camps intent on becoming a super scout. However, the camp itself lost its dreamy sparkle of heroic deeds for me under the yoke of hard work. It was just too much for me, and the food was boring. What was worst of all was that the other boys said rude things like 'bum'. In many ways I was very innocent and very sheltered, and did not have much idea about other people's habits. Desperate not to be branded a sissy, I joined in all the nasty and nefarious exploits that little boys get up to when in packs.

For that camp, out of the kindness of her gentle heart, my mother had made a huge cream cake covered in strawberries. She said that I had to share it. So, like a good little boy, I told the cook, who was a real old battleaxe. Soon the news reached the boys in my tent, and I was in for it. They were furious. How stupid I was for not keeping it for our midnight feast!

So, in order to prove myself one of the boys, I had to set off with an assistant – to make sure I did not cheat – where no scout had ever ventured without permission: to the kitchen to bring back the cake intact! I was reluctant; the poor unfortunate chosen as my assistant was reluctant. Our protests were ignored. So into the pitch black of night we crept, two commandos on our daring culinary raid.

Somehow we got into the kitchen through a window. Long shadows from a cloud-veiled moon were cast into the room, making the stainless-steel sinks and benches shine. The long-bladed knives, so sharp and thin, gleamed with an ominous sheen, and the refrigerator scared us half to death as it clattered into life. And there, in the middle of the work table, glowing like a sacred mountain, stood our prize, the cake! Our enthusiasm overtook us and we both reached out to grab it at the same time – and slipped. The cake rose into the air, as if on wings, and gracefully fell on top of me, while my unfortunate accomplice was covered in eggs and sausages laid out for the morning's breakfast. Saucepans, frying pans and plates clattered to the floor, and we left as fast as we could. But on the way out, we raided the refrigerator and managed to swipe a large opened tin of plums.

Both of us were terrified of what would happen to us once we returned to our tent. But when we told the others our woeful story, we were let off the hook, even winning their admiration. After all, we did nick the plums, so everything was OK. The next morning, the cook appeared at the flap of my tent, wanting to ask us a few questions . . . If walls have ears, it seems that kitchen walls have memories as well.

The Boy Scouts were really great fun, after I learnt how to avoid the camps. I then discovered something even better: the Army Cadets! You could only join if you were fourteen or over, but many of my friends had lied about their age – boys of eleven, twelve and thirteen. I was only eleven when I decided to enlist. So I applied and, to my astonishment, was accepted! I felt like a king for a week.

I couldn't stop boasting to my friends. I told everyone about it, including the rubbishmen, who didn't seem too impressed. When my mother found out, she hit the roof. She was furious. 'Peter, I just don't know what made you go and do a stupid thing like that . . . really!' I did not have a reply. I wanted some excitement, a challenge in life. My father thought I was mad. Eventually my parents relented. At least the uniform was free.

When I arrived on the first night I was rather taken aback by the whole situation. A large hall with a roof and long rafters all in a light green seemed imposing. There was the noise of the arms drill, and unbending discipline. However, I managed to dodge the arms drill and head straight towards the brass band. Glamour, excitement, at last a chance to show off! That is what I was after then, a place in the sun. I was very small compared to the other boys in the band, and I began to regret my decision when I was told that I would be playing the cymbals.

They were huge, brass and very heavy. I was frightened of slicing my nose off with the edge of them each time I had to bang them together. But I soon got the swing of things and was able to clash them in time with the rest of the band. I really enjoyed the uniform, gloves, the busby with the plume. The whole thing appealed to my sense of flair and the dramatic.

I took the band rehearsals very seriously. But the company instructor had a great deal of heartache teaching me how to march. After being told I had two left feet, I was informed countless times (he was losing his patience) that I was out of step. I invented my own system, a kind of breakdancing applied to marching. My bad marching gave everyone the impression that I was crippled. My breakdance marching made me look as if I was having a bad case of the runs, but slowly that progressed to a type of hop and skip which looked more like a Highland fling.

This incurred the wrath of the entire band and caused everyone else hoots of laughter. But one day before bed, in a fit of fevered prayer, I asked that I could be made to march perfectly, and wonder of wonders it happened. Whether it was the prayer, or my ego unable to handle the humiliation, it was of no consequence: I could march in time and keep up with the rest of the band!

Out in parades from then on, I really showed off, twirling the cymbals, clashing them together, announcing my presence to the world. Nicknamed 'Cymbals', I used to get all the jibes that the other band members could throw at me. But I couldn't stand that for very long, so the burning pangs of ambition drove me on. I wanted to become a tenor drummer. I would achieve respect, honour, and at last I would be jibe-free; but, more important, some other poor hapless person would play the cymbals. My bondage would be over.

Everyone complained that I was too small to be a tenor drummer, but I pushed the point, and at last I got my chance. I worked very hard to become good enough to drill, but I was not good enough to go out on parade.

During this time a new band leader had been appointed. He was a burly sergeant, with a large wart on the left side of his cheek just below his nose. His face was pudgy, his smile cruel and his eyes had a rather dull expression to them. His hair looked like an old dishcloth, tired, greasy and lifeless. Psychically I sensed that he and I would run into a rather large spot of bother sooner or later. I sensed that it would be *sooner*.

What was worse, he was a drummer. A tenor drummer. He constantly reminded everyone that he was the best tenor drummer. He had no sense of modesty. Therefore we in the drum section were constantly berated. Everyone was terrified of him. He always swore, so much and so blue you could sharpen a knife on the atmosphere, and he did not like Catholics. I never discovered why. I thought it very strange not to like Catholics. The glorious Pope, Vicar of Christ, and the wonderful Holy Church! Weren't the Catholics the Chosen Ones? They were always the good guys, the Bible was full of them! Wasn't Jesus one? Of course, as I grew up, I realized why there were many people who didn't like Catholics, and all their reasons seemed to be perfectly sound.

This sarcastic sergeant kept goading me because I was Catholic, did not swear (I did not know how) and was not in his eyes a very good drummer. Oh, the trials and tribulations of childhood! But soon I was swearing just like a trooper, but only during band practice.

The day came when I was finally going on parade with the others, and some other little boy had taken up the cymbals. Everyone was getting ready. Panic set in as the rigmarole of making everything perfect consumed the band. The drill hall resounded with the excited voices of young would-be soldiers ready for their first important parade. Suddenly the sergeant, who was band leader for the parade, screamed out in a loud voice, 'Where is that bloody Cymbals – that good-for-nothing new boy?' There was absolute silence.

'Well, where in the world is he? Does anybody know? You, Chambers, do you know where he is?'

'No, sergeant, I don't. Sorry.' As it turned out, he had the good sense not to turn up. I felt something horrible was about to happen, and it was going to happen to me. I felt the sergeant staring at me, mulling over the situation. I distinctly disliked what I felt he was thinking. My stomach began to churn.

'Chambers!'

'Yes, sergeant?' I replied, expecting doom.

'Chambers, go and put the cymbals on now. Your

drumming career will have to wait until some other time.'

Doom struck. I was thunderstruck. I blushed bright red, I felt so insulted! I had fallen into disgrace, from the ranks of a tenor drummer back to a mere cymbals player. Murderous thoughts went out against this other boy. The anger passed, but indignation took its place. So, mustering all my strength, and in my loudest voice, I yelled 'No!'

Disaster! Puberty had beaten me to it – no earthshaking roar but a pathetic high-pitched squeak. Amazingly, though, it had the desired effect.

It was the end of a brilliant musical career. But my friends in the band applauded me for what I had done. My parents were relieved.

Later I discovered that this tyrannical sergeant worked in a shop selling ladies' underwear, which seemed a far cry from the military glory he so often expounded. One day I walked up to his counter and said, 'Hello, sergeant.' As he turned round, his face went a dark crimson – matching a pair of frilly knickers he was holding. I ran off to tell my friends in the band. A child's revenge is worse than poison. Soon after that I heard that he had left the Army Cadets. He had lost the ability to control the band, after being given the nickname 'Sergeant Knickers'.

This whole exercise in military and musical discipline lasted three months, and luckily it was the closest I came to the real thing. I would have had nightmares of a hundred sergeants like old 'Knickers'.

After that, I was a Sea Cadet for three glorious stomach-churning nights and an Air Force Cadet for one – but it was too full of slick young men for me. I also did a quick tour of the youth clubs. At the same time, I became a Young Conservative, which made my father shake his head in disgust; then a Young Liberal; and then, to my father's delight, a Young Socialist. I also became a Young Communist, because they had the best table-tennis table in the neighbourhood, and the best-looking girls. However, I was dragged out of the people's party, by my panic-stricken mother and a gnarled Irish priest who was spitting hellfire and brimstone. It was probably really whisky. My mother looked as if the devil himself had dug his claws into my soul. My involvement with the world of politics lasted, all in all, two weeks.

My most constant childhood activity was that of altar server, prompted by my faith, my mother and my interest in deeper realities. Until I started to think for myself, and discovered that Roy Rogers did not actually write the letters that he sent to me, I was totally addicted to Roman Catholicism, and my piety would have melted the very cross itself. In my robes, I looked as if the communion wafer would not melt in my mouth, and I knew my duties backwards. As a child, one of my most interesting experiences was when I was involved in an Ethiopian Coptic Mass. It was bizarre. An Ethiopian priest was a guest at St Dominic's Priory for some reason, and he belonged to a section of the Coptic Church that had resumed communion with the Roman Catholic Church after a thousand-year separation. Everyone in the congregation wanted to get in on this mass. It was unique, strange, intriguing – and a pleasant break from the normal routine.

It was the first time in the United Kingdom that this had happened; the large church was packed to capacity, even the standing room was filled. The lights went down, the whispers of prayer subsided into reverent

42

silence, the visitor began. No one had any idea what he was saying or even doing half the time, it was so utterly different. The Ethiopian seemed to break out in a cold sweat of devotion and asked for a drum. But alas, there was no drum, so he clapped his hands and stamped his feet. He wanted a surging-up tempo, a divine beat. No one else joined in. The congregation became apprehensive. The priests became apprehensive. I heard someone mutter, 'What's going on? Is this a jazz club or a church?' The visitor continued to get into the swing of things, swaying his hips, making a few ladies gasp. He wailed loudly. The congregation sat stolidly but politely, unsure what to do.

Yet even my pious activities within the House of God were not to last long, due to the tricks of my closest childhood friend, Bernard Nolan. Whenever together, we could never keep a straight face. Trouble of some sort always seemed to crop up. Bernard wanted to join the Guild of Servers and, regardless of his reasons, I knew deep down that this would spell disaster. I, of all people, was appointed to teach him the rules, and that was a big mistake. I had told Bernard that, after the communion, the priest would come along with the chalice, and you had to pour wine over his fingers into the chalice, and then he would drink it. After this was done, the priest would return, and you would pour water and wine into the chalice.

At that point Bernard burst out, 'You mean he staggers back for more!'

I thought that was terribly funny and burst into laughter. That joke was my downfall.

Time passed, and then I was told I would be the one to help Bernard through his first communion. I protested and was told not be silly. The fateful day came and we had the good fortune to secure the most irritable priest that ever graced the earth. His name was Father Wilde and he lived up to his name. He was cranky and nervous and did the entire Mass in twenty minutes.

Some people said that he had gone barmy after performing an exorcism. Even so, he had a brilliant mind, but he was a pain in the neck. Flanking this priest, we approached the altar to respond to the liturgy. Father Wilde proceeded so fast that we made many mistakes, and he'd then stop in mid-service to shout at us. His broad Irish accent echoed all over the church, waking up even those faithful ones who had fallen asleep.

Then came the fateful moment. Father Wilde approached with the chalice. We doled out the wine. He drank it down in one complete swallow. I felt like calling 'Time, gentlemen, please!' Father Wilde returned the second time, and it seemed as if he really was staggering. Instantly I recalled Bernard's comment and, as great minds think alike, he looked at me, I looked at him, and we erupted with laughter. We dropped what we were holding and fell about on the floor, hooting hysterically.

Father Wilde totally flipped. He reacted as if the Second Coming had brought Mohammed instead of Christ. He screamed with rage and shook all over, but the more he yelled, the more we laughed. Thus we were suspended and I never resumed my work for the Lord after that.

But another and just as mysterious attraction took its place: girls!

Bernard had twin sisters, and to me at that time they seemed all that is perfect in a woman. Josephine and Margaret brought lumps to my throat, but it was Margaret who had the special allure. I had a terrible crush on her, which I thought I kept secret, but to everyone else it was painfully obvious.

On one sweltering occasion at Bernard's house, I could not believe my luck, when I found myself alone with her. So I suggested that she reveal one or two of her attractions. Such things had heretofore remained purely mythical to me. She only took off her jumper, but to my fevered imagination anything was possible. I was not sure what to do in any case, but I had gleaned a stock of phrases from the local cinema. Just as I said 'Hey baby, let's get together, just the two of us right now', her father walked in.

I had never moved so fast in my life. He chased me all around his living-room, cursing me loudly, and then all the way home. Thank God he did not catch me. I might have ended up stuffed above the Nolan mantel-piece. By the next day, Mr Nolan had calmed down, but Bernard teased me about it for weeks.

In later life, Margaret went on to become a well-known actress.

All through this period, questions from deep inside me concerning death and the mysteries of life began to surface again, and I was constantly brought back to two of the most striking experiences of my early childhood.

When I was young, I constantly overheard the mysterious expression 'dying'. This word remained a complete enigma to me, especially after asking people its meaning and not receiving a satisfactory reply. So I put the question to one side and went about my life like any normal child. But queries about death came back inevitably. I had seen dead birds on the street, and people on the bus often spoke about it – the whole thing seemed very confusing.

On the corner of Malden Road, less than five minutes' walk from my house, was the neighbourhood shop. It was an old-fashioned corner shop but also a dairy. For some reason, this shop had always been run by Welsh people, and at that time the owner was a Mr Richards.

He was an impressively tall Welshman. I had never seen anyone so big before, and so he made me slightly nervous. He was gruff and quite reserved, but once you got to know him he had a heart of gold. He ran his shop impeccably. It was spotlessly clean and he was always willing to extend a little credit – only a little, mind you – if times were hard. Every morning he would come round promptly at 8.30 to deliver the milk. He would ladle it out of churns into pails, for the newfangled milk bottle had not yet come to my part of London. After going from door to door, ladling out the fat of the land, Mr Richards knew all the juicy gossip, and started some of the more saucy rumours himself.

One day I was honoured and trusted with the momentous task of delivering the shopping list to Mr Richards. Although it was not far to go, I ran all the way. The shop was full when I arrived, so I had to wait my turn. Being a very inquisitive child, I used to study people, and eventually found myself overhearing a conversation between two old ladies. It shook me to my very core.

This conversation changed me from a happy-go-lucky five-year-old into a frightened little boy in a matter of seconds. As they rambled on, I heard distinctly the shocking sentence: 'And fancy her just up and dying like that! Leaving those two children alone, without a mother.' These last words scrambled my brain. Tears engulfed me as I ran home in blind panic, still clutching the shopping list. The journey seemed to take for ever, no matter how fast I ran. As I crashed through the back door, I thought, 'Is this going to happen to my mother . . . to *me*?'

It took a full hour before I could speak coherently and explain what had happened. My tears dwindled as the soothing love of my mother calmed me down, and the words slowly trickled out. I told her about the terrible conversation I had overheard, then, looking right up into her clear blue eyes, asked imploringly, 'It's not true, is it, Mummy? Tell me it's not. You won't die before me, will you?' She looked at me and smiled. I grabbed her arm. 'People don't really die, do they, Mummy? I won't, will I?'

My mother was a very sensible woman. Holding me close, she simply said, 'Yes, darling, it will happen to me, to you, to Daddy, to everyone. It's part of God's plan. But it won't happen to us for a long, long time yet.'

She held me close for a time and then set me down, and happily but wistfully I wandered out into the back garden. The world had become a very different place: the colours had more depth to them, the air shimmered. I sat down on the garden steps. Nature was trying to talk to me. I looked up at the sky and found myself becoming lost in its blue expanse. Peace washed through me. I listened carefully to the wind as it brushed through the trees.

I began, in my childish way, to wonder just how I knew things before they happened, or could see and hear things that other people could not, sensing presences from the spirit world. It was to be sixteen long years of soul-searching before I finally discovered the answer.

My mother came out into the garden and sat beside me. A question came to me but, before I had a chance to ask it, as if she had read my mind, she smiled and said, 'Yes, Peter, it will be almost like forever. Only our bodies will pass away.'

She then stood up and left me alone with that thought. I watched the wind blow the dead leaves from the trees on to the grass, and a quiet joy flooded through me. Intimations of eternity flickered before me. I felt the spirit within me for the first time; and for a second I saw Creation's light and I knew that there was no death.

My seventh year also marked a major turning-point in my life. Early one cold winter's morning, I was woken from my sleep by someone calling my name, but it seemed as if the voice was far away. As I woke, I saw my grandmother, my father's mother, by the side of my bed. She was smiling warmly, happy to see me. I was surprised to see her there at such a strange hour – she lived sixty miles away. Then I noticed a most beautiful silvery-blue light around her, which gradually changed into shimmering gold. And there was a perfume in the air. Her presence made me feel strange.

'What are you doing here, Grandma?' I asked curiously.

'To say hello, but also goodbye, Peter. I know that you've been worried about dying. I died four hours ago.'

I wasn't shocked; it seemed to make sense somehow.

'There's no need to be afraid of death, Peter. You can see that I'm still alive, but in another way.'

We talked for some time, and slowly she faded away.

'Grandma, tell me where you're going,' I pleaded. But she was gone. I looked at the clock. It was five in the morning. I peered out of the window through flurries of snow, hoping to see her. I ran out into the hallway hoping to find her, but at the bottom of the staircase stood my parents. The telephone was dangling in Father's hand.

'Did you see Grandma too?' I asked excitedly. They looked shocked. 'She just told me she was dead,' I added proudly.

My parents were astonished. A family friend had just telephoned to tell them that my grandmother had died four hours earlier.

Later I went back into my room, buzzing with energy. Somehow, at that young age, I knew my clairvoyance had come to stay. A winter's sun was rising faintly. With the hardship of winter, when things seemed to die, the promise of new life and the understanding of the human spirit struck home vividly. I watched the sun rise, and then fell asleep, peaceful and content.

At the funeral I didn't cry, because I knew she was happy.

Chapter 3
The Coffee-Bar Kid

My adolescent years and early twenties were packed with as much excitement, experience and energy as I could muster. I lived as if only the moment existed. Often my experiences seemed to conflict with each other, from psychic to physical, emotional to mystical. The world often seemed in a dizzy spin. But in the end I began to see how all my experiences fitted into one large jigsaw puzzle, allowing me to use my psychic abilities in many different ways.

During my childhood years I had read a lot of ghost stories as well as stories with unexplained mysteries. I was thoroughly intrigued by ghosts – what they were, why they existed. I wanted to know if they could communicate anything to the living. Early on I began to see ghosts, mainly victims of the Blitz, and it was quite natural when I reached my teens that a-ghost-hunting I would go. I went on a few such expeditions but did not see very much at all, and became rather disappointed with the whole idea, thinking that my psychic abilities had failed. Then a friend suggested we should try somewhere very old, with a mixed and varied history. So off we went to camp overnight in that beautiful place, Epping Forest. The forest is haunted by hundreds of unfortunate earth-bound souls all roaming around trying to get some message across. At night or in the early evening it can be truly spooky.

Once we got to the forest we proceeded for about half an hour under tall, graceful trees. The ground was muddy with the imprints of horses as we walked along a bridle path, and finally we came to a small pond in the heart of a copse. This was the place. I could feel the atmosphere. It vibrated with ghostly presence. This copse was regarded by the locals as the most haunted area of the forest. For some reason the spot seemed particularly to attract earth-bound spirits who had met with tragic deaths. Its history went back way before the Middle Ages, so of course a lot had happened, and those events were etched firmly in the energy of the place.

We set up camp, made an evening meal and waited until we both felt the time was right to hunt for ghosts. I sensed that we should walk around the pond to the far side of the copse. The sky was clear that night, the air crisp and biting. Much to my surprise a full moon suddenly rose just above us, looking as though it was resting on the treetops. It seemed to be watching us. Everything was quiet; only the thud of our footsteps could be heard. We came to that part of the copse where I felt the hunt would be most worthwhile. I began to feel I was being watched by many pairs of eyes. I sensed undefined shapes around me – so did my friend, to whom the idea of ghost-hunting had suddenly lost its appeal.

I felt we should move even further into the copse. Suddenly I stopped dead, for on the clear night air we could hear the sound of church bells tolling, deep and resonant. I nearly panicked, then got control of myself when I realized there was a church just under half a mile away. We both laughed, and continued our search for the supernatural mysteries of Epping Forest.

We explored the area further, but nothing seemed to happen. After about an hour of what seemed to be a fruitless enterprise, we decided to go back to the tent. Dejected and hopes quashed, we started back. Just as we reached the top of a small rise, we saw, directly in our path, a mysterious blue light. We both thought it was marsh gas and moved on. We had proceeded for about twenty minutes, when I sensed something was walking a few paces behind us. All types of wild thoughts rushed through my mind. Was this a ghost? The spectre of a murderer? How long had it been following us? Then came the thought . . . perhaps it was a real-life murderer! Terrified, I stopped in my tracks. My friend was still walking, and turned to ask why I had stopped. But as he turned, his mouth dropped open. His eyes bulged. Gingerly I turned, and there before us stood a ghost – a very old monastic figure who seemed to be looking right through us at something else. The figure began to move towards us, and both my friend and I yelled in fright! In our rush to get away, we fell over each other into the mud. But with that ghost right behind us, we took off hell for leather back to the camp.

As previously agreed, we did not speak about what we had seen. First we wrote it down, so as to compare notes.

Interestingly, we both came up with the same conclusion – that the ghost was not particularly inter- ested in the two of us, and was probably only superficially aware of our presence. It seemed totally preoccupied with something else. Perhaps a memory from centuries past. My appetite for psychic knowledge grew immensely after that, but so did my caution and discernment, I am happy to say.

To see a ghost, as I later learned, is nothing to boast about.

After that experience, a lot of psychic knowledge about how to use my gifts emerged of its own accord. I discovered that I did not need to go in search of it. These abilities were already there within me, and so was the inherent knowledge about operating and using it. I learnt how to predict sequences of events to a time scale, and to refine my ability of seeing into the future.

The school I enjoyed most in lots of ways was the technical school I attended until I was eighteen. I was always involving myself in mad pranks and one of the most amusing entirely stupid things that I ever did there was the sabotage of Mrs Piggott's bicycle. Mrs Piggott was the ever-suffering school secretary. She used to cycle through Camden Town to Hampstead each day, returning by the same route. Always the butt of practical jokes, Mrs Piggott was a prime target for the mischievous amongst the school's ranks, which was about ninety-nine per cent of the school population!

So I, along with some other rascals, decided to remove her brakes. The next day our headmaster, a warlike Welshman, Mr Jones, appeared like a Titan on the platform, resplendent in his own glory. He stood still for a moment, staring round the entire assembly, fuming with anger. Then he began to roar. 'You dirty dogs!' Someone in the assembly howled, someone else barked. A breeze of laughter ran through the crowd. Mr Jones continued, 'Those revolting boys amongst you – yes, you know who I mean – who sabotaged poor Mrs Piggott's bicycle, I want you all, *now*!' Because of his strong Welsh accent, his voice went a little haywire when he reached boiling point. Eight hundred young boys crashed into hysterical laughter. Absolute bedlam broke loose and, of course, Mr Jones went completely off his rocker. In order to get his point across, our hypertense headmaster went on to explain in detail Mrs Piggott's journey of horror down Camden High Street. When she saw a red light, she tried to apply her brakes. Alas, poor Mrs Piggott could only scream with terror when she found she could not stop! Gallantly, she weaved her way through oncoming traffic and past a bus, with her heart in her mouth. Normally it was on her sleeve. On and on the headmaster ranted, recounting the unfortunate plight of Mrs Piggott, which only served to add to our delight. Then came the fateful warning: unless the despicable culprits came forward and owned up, the whole school would be punished. So all of us involved did the decent thing and took our punishment. And for about fours weeks after that memorable event, my bottom felt as if it had a headache. Mrs Piggott was subsequently very wary of me when I smiled at her, and she never rode her bicycle again.

I had a great sense of urgency to get through school and end my adolescence. Germany seemed the ideal place to go next. It was not long before I found myself on the bustling streets of Düsseldorf, which was to become my home for two years. I gained greatly from being involved with another culture which, while so similar to my own, was also vastly different. I stayed in a hostel run by a Roman Catholic priest, a likeable rogue who had worked against the Nazis. Behind the altar in his living-room, the push of a secret button and a silent turn revealed a bar jam-packed with spirits of all kinds to give solace and comfort, if the more orthodox spirit was no use.

The school I attended in Germany was called a 'Gymnasium', and it was rather like a senior college or branch of a university. The education I so gladly received there was very good and very demanding. I had quite a good time on the whole, and studied European History and Philosophy, which served to broaden my outlook on the world immensely.

My enthusiasm for the great outdoors really came to its apex when I was in Germany. I spent a great deal of time in outings to the countryside and in mountaineering. One mountain that was my favourite is called the Drachenfels. One day I was filled with anticipation of climbing the north face, and I was determined I should get to the top unhindered. After about thirty-five minutes I was half way up – about eight hundred feet from the bottom. Suddenly I slipped. I grabbed at what I thought was a rock, but in fact was nothing more than solidified rubble. Of course this broke in my hands and I began to fall helter-skelter down the hard granite cliff-face. I grabbed for a bush, but it too came away in my hand, and I came to fear that my time on earth was up.

Then came that often-quoted sensation of seeing all that has taken place in one's life. Everything of importance and everything minor seemed to pass before me. All the unseen causes and effects of my thoughts and actions also revealed themselves, and within came a silent prayer. I felt at peace, and waited for the final impact; it would be quick, I thought, no pain at least . . . But fortunately on the way I hit a telephone post. I was badly winded, but the post broke my fall and I landed in a heap with nearly all my skin left up on the mountain side. Someone up above must have had some regard for me.

I lay there on my back, winded and bleeding. My

vision was blurry and muddled; the clouds high above me were a whirling mass of white. Voices crowded around me, gasps and sighs of concern. My raw flesh ached. The agony was settling in. Somewhere I heard an ambulance approaching, its siren of rescue. I felt there was someone close to me, one of the climbers, Hans. He began to talk to me, giving words of encouragement. One of the girls in the group began to sob. Some of the others thought I was going to die. I prayed. How I prayed that I would live, that this was just some horrible nightmare, that the accident was not true! The ambulance came to a screeching halt.

Reassuringly, the ambulancemen lifted me on to a special stretcher and into the vehicle. I felt my friends crowding around me, wishing me well. I blacked out, but for how long I had no idea. Yet within the turbulence of my mind, I felt a strong pull, a psychic tug. My astral body came free, and there before me was the tunnel of light, the great gateway to the spirit world. People I had never met before welcomed me with open arms. There my grandmother gave me a smile of love. Closer and closer I came to the spirit world – and the closer I came, the more I wanted to stay there. The material world seemed like a childhood dream, distant, innocent, no longer important. A great sense of euphoria swept through me. It felt just like the first time I had ever been kissed by a girl. My grandmother's outstretched hand was just inches from my grasp, when suddenly I was snapped back to reality.

My eyes fluttered open. Above me hovered the concerned face of the doctor. 'You're lucky to be alive. No bones broken. You have concussion, but it won't last long. You will need a few skin grafts, but soon your skin will grow back and you'll be just like new again, OK?' I nodded, and smiled weakly, falling back into a deep sleep. The drugs I was given had numbed me to the outside world.

Germany gave me a chance to develop my independence. The Germans' solid example of rebuilding their country and leaving the past behind gave me a great deal of inspiration as to how I should approach my own life.

It was a time of new vibrant forms of music and art and my awareness was on the verge of exploding into new and greater understanding; there was more to the world than I had realized. Life was not as simple as I had thought. Where did all these new ideas germinate? In my favourite environment, the coffee-bar. In its smoky underground sub-culture I began to meet like-minded people. To most young people today, a coffee-bar is no more than a place where you go to have a cup of coffee after a late show, or merely to fill in time. But not so in the late fifties and early sixties! Then the world swung to rock and roll. There was rising affluence after the shock of the war, and young people everywhere were out for a good time. Polite society classified coffee-bars as dens of immorality, lairs of sexual licence, drug-taking, subversive political ideas and weird Eastern religions. They were thought of as the knife that would cut apart the very fabric of responsible society. As far as drugs were concerned the most readily available was black, bitter and powdery, infused with water to become that pleasing stimulant – strong dark espresso coffee consumed in huge amounts by the youth of the day.

They were marvellous places, where whole cross-sections of society could meet on equal terms. Often the future of the world was excitably discussed with burning but naive passion.

Because these fantastic places inspired me, I used to do impromptu readings for my friends. One such time was when a girl I knew came over and asked me to help her. Her mother seemed on her deathbed, and the girl desperately wanted to know the whereabouts of her father, since he had left them both years before. This pretty young girl had only vague childhood memories of him, and she had tried to gain more information from her mother – but she was far too sick to reply. I realized the importance of her need, and, though I was still relatively inexperienced, I concentrated hard. Vibrations came to me as I fingered this girl's watch. North, the direction *north*. I told her that she would find him somewhere in North London. Then I got a street number and, vaguely, the name of the street. But the reading changed of its own accord: I saw an image of this same girl taking her father to the mother's bedside. Then I saw a rush of time, and the mother was better, and both parents were reunited! I couldn't wholly believe what I'd just seen – and it was such a gamble to reveal it to the distressed girl, in case I turned out to be wrong. I certainly did not want to raise her hopes over nothing. Yet something inside me urged me to tell her – and I told her everything. She appraised me hard with searching eyes, thanked me and left. I sighed nervously, hoping I'd done the right thing.

A month later I bumped into her, once again in the same coffee-bar. As she grabbed me I thought, 'Oh, God, I'm in for it now!' But instead she gave me a kiss. She had found her father just as I had said. Furthermore her mother was now on the mend, and her parents were even talking of getting back together. A week later, this same very happy girl was killed in a motorcycle accident. Her parents did remarry.

For a short time I was a coffee-bar psychic, and I

learnt a lot about relating to people. It was a far cry from the youth clubs that I knew, where the priest would gently but firmly grab you by the cuff and introduce you to young stuffed-shirt men and nice girls who looked as though they were doing character profiles of the Virgin Mary! I regarded myself as an adventurous person and I did not want to know only young people who hung on to the apron-strings of the Church. My life was going to be exciting, out of the ordinary. Such were the dreams of the sixteen-year-old psychic. Little did I realize just how right those early dreams would turn out to be.

We used to dance around demonstrating, but on the whole my generation were clean-cut and quite innocent. The streets would resound to the chants of 'Ho! Ho! Ho Chi Minh! We shall fight and we shall win!' But fight for what? Most of us had no idea. Another fashionable chant was 'Hey, hey, LBJ! How many kids have you killed today?' and often in our unbridled enthusiasm we would believe this to be true. I stood outside the American Embassy like anyone else doing their bit, but if I had analysed what I was doing at the time, I would have realized it was a complete waste of our energy.

At that time I was politically involved, in a very minor way, with the Committee of One Hundred – the civil disobedience division of the anti-nuclear movement. I was then, and still am, opposed to nuclear arms, for they can burn a path of destruction and desolation for all mankind. We have the power of creating the solutions to a nuclear-free future, if only we can learn to understand nature.

In my youth I was very much 'ban the bomb', and I often expected to be carried away and arrested, but I never was.

One coffee-bar which became a haunt of mine was

the Witch's Cauldron. It was the 'in' place and in those days a young man called Wally Whiteman, now a television presenter, was making a name for himself as a folk-singer. When he sang in the Cauldron, the place would be packed out. He sang haunting songs with great intensity, creating an atmosphere exciting to be in. He was free to say things through his songs that he could not say on the BBC. He sang stirring revolutionary songs of the Welsh miners, and their plaintive lyrics would echo softly round that crowded coffee-bar.

Another coffee-bar I frequented was called the Loft. It was rather more daring and had a more intense atmosphere than the Cauldron, but it was not as friendly. The police were forever raiding it for being open after hours. I look back on those days with a little bit of pride, a great deal of pleasure and a few twinges of embarrassment.

My psychic faculties began to start maturing around this time, so I wanted to find practical ways of putting them to good use. All those hours that I spent sitting in coffee-bars helped nourish my spirit and showed me what to re-evaluate within my life. During this time the major re-evaluation was my relationship with my parents. My father was a hardworking man who did the best he could for his family on a material level. He and I had hardly anything in common. I was just a cocky teenager, a product of the post-war society, and I lived in an environment substantially different from the one my father had known. My father had a tendency to dwell on the struggles of the war, and regarded the hardship that we all went through as being good for us, but then he understood things about that period and the sufferings people experienced that I never could. Our religious differences grew wider, especially as my interest moved towards the psychic. This was totally beyond his experience; at least he could relate to the Roman Catholic religion, nominally. He was in many ways far more enlightened than I was – he was a quiet man and thought very deeply but seldom said much. He was compassionate at heart, but I used to goad him unnecessarily. Looking back, this was a stupid thing to do. To me, my father seemed like a red rag to a bull. He was strict, but then he had to be. He would apply the rod so as not to spoil the child, but he would never go overboard in handing out punishment.

I was abroad when my father died, so I could not attend his funeral. He passed away quickly – it took only three days and he was gone. The only funeral that I have attended was my mother's. In some ways I had tried to exclude him from my life, but now I do have regrets that I never understood my father better.

Trafalgar Square was filled with the hustle and bustle of the demonstration. Around me, the echoing voices of the speakers startled thousands of pigeons into flight. The great bronze lions seemed totally unmoved by our youthful pleas to humanity, as did the governments that we were protesting to. The clouds were thick and heavy, and a dark bronze light shimmered in the sky. It was the approach of a winter's evening, and the atmosphere was so strange that it seemed that Nelson might any moment rise from his column and fly away.

Cheers and cries of agreement welled through the crowd as clichés were applauded yet again. The demonstrators were like leaves in a huge tree, set off into rustling and murmuring by the wind of dissent and opinion.

This huge volatile crowd was held together by one word: peace. A single human wish, an aspiration of the ages, since mankind first became dissatisfied with his lot. It was fragile and ambiguous like that other word, death. It seemed to me that peace and death were fingers on the same hand.

There I stood amongst this surging crowd, on the eve of my twenty-first birthday. The day when society was traditionally supposed to accept you as a responsible adult. To be attending an anti-establishment rally – saying no to the powers that be – seemed ironic.

The demonstration marched to the Houses of Parliament, but as time went on the crowds faded away. I rang my home to inform my parents that I would be home later than expected, and to apologize.

The telephone rang and rang; I began to wonder why no one was home – had something happened? Just as I was about to hang up, someone picked up the receiver. It was my younger sister, Pauline, then seventeen.

'Hello, Pauline, it's Peter here. Could you tell Mum and Dad that – '

She interrupted me, her voice sounding tense. 'Peter, prepare yourself for a bit of a shock.'

'What do you mean, Pauline?' I said, expecting nothing in particular.

Pauline hesitated and then I knew it was serious.

'Peter . . . it's Mummy – she's – she's had a stroke! She's gone to the hospital. Dad's with her now . . . I don't know what to do, Peter.'

I told her to stay at home, and that I would be with her as soon as I could. I felt as though I had been stabbed to the heart. I was only twelve or so when I used to pray fervently to the gods above that my mother would not die before me. I hoped that we could die together – a simultaneous death. I was so close to her that our love seemed a bond which welded us together. Perhaps this attitude was almost unhealthy, but for me my mother was a bastion of strength, courage, morality and unassuming saintliness. Now this bastion had collapsed – my prayers had been ignored.

I drove like a madman all the way home. Pauline fell into my arms sobbing uncontrollably. The nightmare had begun. This was going to be a seven-year silent scream, for every minute of every day and every night.

My mother had taken my father to a bingo game. Apparently she was quite lucky and won a few pounds for herself each week. My father hated the whole idea of bingo, but this particular night, she had managed to drag him along too. But all the excitement proved too much for her and she suffered a stroke.

She spent three long months in hospital, agonizing for her, just as agonizing for me and the rest of the family. When I saw her the day after her stroke, I was still in a deep state of shock and disbelief that this could happen to her, of all people. She was very drowsy, and slept fitfully. I came close to her bedside, careful not to disturb her, and held her hand for some time, just pouring energy into her with my mind and willpower. Slowly she opened her eyes, smiled faintly, and weakly said, 'Hello.' Then she drifted back into semi-consciousness.

It was the first time I had ever seen anyone in this state, and it cut me to the quick. The sight of my mother in this condition was almost too much for me to bear. She was bruised black and blue, and a cold fury swept through me. Crazily I grabbed the poor doctor – who managed to calm me down before I hit him. He explained it was not his fault and that he was doing his best. Feeling an absolute idiot, I began to pray for my mother's recovery. Eventually she came out of hospital and began to live at home again, but she was never quite the same again.

She was kept on drugs for the rest of the time she was alive, but they had a terrible side-effect. These drugs made her hallucinate, and she found it difficult to tell reality from hallucination. This disturbed her family, creating tensions that would often escalate into arguments. My father was always by her side, and was incredibly patient with her. Due to the lack of oxygen supplied to her brain, her hallucinations worsened and she often seemed very remote from other people and their company.

For seven long years – remember, life does move in seven-year cycles – this tension was around me. Psychically I found myself tuning in to her pain and suffering. In my ears there was a constant humming sound. I sensed and often experienced her moods and pain. There was no way, it seemed, that I could turn off my awareness of her suffering. It was starting to get to me, turning me into somebody else, some other person that I did not want to be.

One evening, to try and take my mind off it, I went to the cinema. It was 4 July, Independence Day for the United States, but also in a bizarre and ironic fashion, it would be independence day for me. The day of freedom from my mother's pain.

I tried my best to involve myself in the film, and in the excellent acting of Sir John Mills, and, thanks to him, for a while I was lost in the fantasy of the silver screen. As the film came to an end and the house lights gently came to life, throwing their pink and blue glow, I suddenly realized that the noise in my ears had gone. The sensation of tremendous pressure had lifted. Then I felt deeply sad, for I knew this could mean only one thing: Mother was dead.

Still I did not want to believe it as I rushed out into the street and drove home. I was living there at the time and all the fond memories of the past I had shared with her came out, it seemed, to haunt me. I walked into the house; she was not there. Her spirit had left her body. She was gone into a higher realm. My father was sitting slumped in a chair. Pauline was comforting him. He looked shocked, dejected, confused. The inevitable question came.

'Dad, where's Mother?'

He looked at me and knew that I knew.

'She's passed on!' I never quite forgave him for the abrupt way in which he told me, yet I already knew it was true. My mind was confused and irrational for a while. Reality had placed its heavy hand on my weak shoulders and had given me a mighty shove. My father repeated his message in a monotone, 'She's passed on!' This time I felt he was trying to convince himself. The words were still too much for me to accept. I stood as if nailed to the floor.

Then the words poured out of me: 'No, Dad, stop it! You're joking . . . aren't you? You wouldn't joke about that, would you?' But I knew he would not, and I stormed off into the other room, raging with anger on the outside but crumbling inside with a grief that went beyond words. For a second, I cursed being alive. Finally pulling myself together, I lit a cigarette. An inner voice said this grief was nothing but a passing cloud. I dismissed it. I was in no mood for advice.

I began to pace up and down. My mind raced at full speed, trying to comprehend the full implications of my mother's death. It was as if a part of me was dead. I thought back to that time in childhood when she first tried to explain death to me as best she could. Now she, of all people, was gone and it seemed as if death had turned into a giant scorpion, and this scorpion had implanted its sting firmly in my soul. It wasn't bloody fair! I knew that in time I would heal, and my spirit within would have been taught a greater understanding of life through my mother's death. But all that seemed so distant. I was caught between calm and chaos.

I sat by the window looking out into the night. My face was a mask of despair as I gazed at my reflection in the window pane. The house was quiet: everyone was occupied with their own thoughts. It was pitch-black outside, and the glow of my cigarette cast a faint red light over my face. *Mother was finally free of suffering.* The night was so quiet it seemed as if this single thought was broadcast all over London.

Habits die slowly, and often for some time afterwards I would expect to meet her in the street or find her walking through the house. Often I have felt her very close to me. Love goes on for ever. The spirit always ascends, and death is nothing more than another form of birth.

Chapter 4
Mr Benjamin and the White Temple

My early twenties was the most important period in my life. My interest in all things psychic began to become genuine and intelligent. This was prompted in some ways by my mother's long illness and the possibility that it might kill her. From the time I was twenty-three until I was twenty-eight, when my mother eventually died, I was more in search of a deeper reality and awareness than at any other time in my life. I wanted to expand my already strong psychic abilities.

The search for enlightenment was on: the perennial search that has obsessed humanity. It is, I suppose, the desire to know what makes us what we truly are. The discovery of your real *identity* – in other words that which makes you unique, free, and in harmony with life. The true individual behind the name, the job, the wife, the husband, the children, the golf club, what brand of cigarettes you smoke, or what type of clothes you wear, employed or unemployed. The essential you.

Due to my staunch Roman Catholic upbringing, I often had to fight inbuilt prejudices, for Catholics generally regard all psychic things with pity and subtle condescension. Yet, in many of the vivid Bible stories that I was so enthusiastically brought up on, they talk of clairvoyance, mediumship and other psychic skills in very positive ways! Nevertheless I approached the subject with caution, especially aware that my family would not approve.

When I was twenty-three the curiosity of youth took me to a meeting given by one of the truly great mediums of all time, Joe Benjamin. He never had great fame, nor did he want it. He was a quiet man, but the good work he did made many hundreds of people happy, thankful to be alive and more aware of the psychic side of life. I now wanted to know how someone with more experience used his gift.

The meeting was a quiet, almost casual affair. Joe Benjamin pointed at a man in the audience, and asked if he knew anyone called Arthur Haines. 'I have a message for you, sir, from Arthur. He wants to tell you that he is fine, everything is OK, and for you not to worry, as everything that happened in the last month is going to turn out far better than you ever expected.'

Arthur Haines was a well-known comedian who had recently died, and it transpired that the man Joe Benjamin was talking to had been a lifelong friend of Haines. He was Bert Weedon, the well-known guitarist. Haines and Weedon had shared a deep and abiding interest in spiritualism.

I do sincerely believe that there are, unfortunately, many people who *delude* themselves into thinking that they are mediums or psychics. But without a shadow of doubt, Joe Benjamin was the real McCoy. During this truly uplifting demonstration of psychic perception, he also helped a man who was in great distress over the health of his son. This man had broken down into fitful sobbing, for the child, who was only seven or so, was in hospital with a brain tumour.

With one of the boy's handkerchiefs that the father had brought along, Benjamin used psychometry, then consulted his spirit guides. The whole atmosphere of the hall changed as Joe began to tune in to the sick child. Joe's words stay with me even now.

'Don't worry, Mr J, little Alan is going to be quite OK.' Joe concentrated some more as he made further contact with invisible but potent forces. Then he opened his eyes and continued, 'Your son is going to live, regardless of what the doctors say. The doctors are wrong. My spirit guides assure you that he will live to a ripe old age. So don't worry too much. He'll be quite OK.'

Joe Benjamin had the nickname of being the 'quite OK' man, as it seemed to be his favourite saying. The distressed father broke down again into sobs of joy and thanks. Later I discovered that the boy did in fact recover totally.

From that experience I began to gain greater confidence in my own abilities, and I began to care less and less about what other people thought about my involvement with the psychic world. My new-found faith in myself improved my psychic skills dramatically, so I began to experiment in the various ways I could apply my abilities. But in the end, like a horse to water, it always came back to prediction.

Just after the death of my mother, I searched desperately for peace of mind and comfort. I attended a few spiritualist churches but found nothing there of any real use to me: just dry and dusty dogma. In the end, I felt like giving up and letting myself sink into the depression that I was trying to control and keep on top of. As things transpired – perhaps through the influences of higher forces – I ended up attending the White Temple, a spiritualist church in Dagenham village.

I was in desperate need of contacting my mother. I

just wanted to hear from her, to know how she was. Strangely, I received far more than I desired, and it was through a truly good and loving medium called Helen, who was president of the White Temple, that I was helped to overcome my grief. Helen was Jewish, and she had been converted to Christian Spiritualism some years before, but she and her church were far more universal in their attitudes and approach. Helen's husband Paul was a very good healer who exuded a great sense of inner well-being and tranquillity.

They were a happy middle-aged couple who were very much in love, as was obvious to the rest of the world. Their love was spontaneous and constant. Indirectly each of them added another dimension of improvement and maturity to my psychic abilities through their kindness, advice and personal example. Helen taught me always to question people who professed to be mediums or psychics, especially if they claimed to have messages from the spirit world. Even now I encourage my clients to question me if they are unsure about anything, no matter how small or seemingly unimportant. After all I, like any clairvoyant, medium or psychic, am giving nothing more than a psychic opinion – until circumstance can back up what I have predicted. Then, and only then, does my psychic opinion become psychic fact. Fortunately I am hardly ever wrong.

Helen was a large lady, and she exuded a very motherly and candid approach to life, endowed with wisdom and great foresight. She became a very real source of inspiration to me as I went through my time of grief. Through her influence I received a great healing, and an immediate example of how a real psychic works. Intelligently and unselfishly, Helen used her skills in a total and powerful way. Many people owe her a great deal for the help she gave them. She gave me love, when I most needed it.

Three years later, when I was in Birmingham, I visited another White Temple, in search of something similar, I suppose. But what I ended up with was totally unexpected and, at first, totally unwelcome!

As I walked into this temple, the organ was playing quietly and the place had a very serious atmosphere. I found a seat in the back row and waited until the formalities of addressing the congregation were over. Something had told me to pay special attention to the demonstration of mediumship that would follow.

There were at least two hundred people in the church hall that night. Most of them were eager for a message of some sort, I suppose. Quite a few people received rather ordinary messages, and I began to regret that I had come at all. Just as I was thinking about leaving at the next opportunity, the rather stern-looking medium, probably in her late eighties, pointed her finger at me! I thought that she must have a message from my mother.

People in the rows in front of me turned around. I did not know what to do with all those faces staring at me!

'Young man, yes you, now don't hide in the corner like that! Yes, I know you think I'm old. I am, but I can still see you. Stand up so I can get a good clear look at you!'

So I stood up. I felt as if I was back in school. I smiled weakly.

The medium scrutinized me with a rather imperious look, then said matter-of-factly, 'Young man, you will be doing what I am now doing. It will happen all of its own accord, and when you least expect it. Stronger forces than you can imagine are guiding your destiny. Yes, you will help many, many people in a very big

71

way.' I was about to protest when she continued, 'I know you don't believe me, but you wait and see. Time will prove me right . . . oh, and by the way, your mother says for goodness sake will you stop worrying about her and start getting on with your life!'

I sat down, feeling a trifle overpowered by all this. I didn't want to be any kind of full-time psychic, not at that point. *I* certainly was not going to be prancing around the stage giving messages from those in the spirit world! How wrong I turned out to be! Of course, in time I put out of my mind that lady's little prophecy, and just got on with my life. But like a thunderbolt, it came back to me a few months after I had started to work as a psychic, and I was amazed at how I had ignored the obvious.

One night I could not sleep and it was really pouring down outside. The house that I was living in at the time had a broken gutter, and water would cascade down across my bedroom window, making a waterfall of reflected night-time images. As I lay in bed, smoking my cigarette, and watching the smoke form into magical shapes, I felt as if I was being watched. There were eyes somewhere, looking at me. Instinctively I turned to the window, where the cascade of water fell with a veil-like effect. My worry about not having enough money to live on had been nagging away in the pit of my stomach. As I looked at the window, from out of this watery sheen came a single point of light which began to form itself into a face. Then the atmosphere in the bedroom grew extremely still. My dog Bonce lifted his head, intrigued by what he was seeing. Yes, animals see people from the spirit world, too.

I stared at this face, thinking that it must just be

nothing more than my imagination working under stress, or lack of sleep. But then the face in the window spoke to me.

I almost dropped my cigarette! Bonce barked, thumping his tail on the floor.

'Peter, I am your guide, to help you through this difficult time. This is a time of testing. You have a long and hard path to travel. Those of us in the spirit world know that you are worried by money.'

That was certainly true!

'You will always have enough, but the time will come when you will have money in abundance. Then you must share it wisely.'

Before I had a chance to ask any questions, the face faded back into the streaming water, as if washed into oblivion. I was absolutely amazed at what had just happened. Then I realized that my sense of worry had gone. I was no longer tense about not having money, because I knew that I would always be given enough. I fell asleep then – but suddenly woke in a panic. The cigarette! Where was the bloody cigarette? I had images of the whole place burning down. I was so dazed by sleep that I did not notice it in my other hand. I had fallen asleep with it still burning. I said 'Thank you' aloud for being woken up. As soon as I said that, I clairaudiently heard, *'That's all right. Just be more careful in future.'* I smiled. Someone in the spirit world cared enough to save my life.

Clairaudience is one of my gifts that I use a lot in consultations with clients. Blending my ability to do psychometry with clairvoyance, I am often told important things by those in the spirit world. The world is full of unseen people. The houses and flats that we live in, we share with invisible guests. Often when I go out for a quiet drink down at the local pub, I am gently amused by watching people having conversations, while people from the spirit world are listening in. They are not eavesdroppers really; it is just that some spirit people like to mix in with people.

Similarly, if I go for a walk in Hyde Park, I often see people from the last century wandering around, taking their dogs for a walk, or watching the ducks. Once I had a conversation with a gentleman who had been terribly upset about the death of Queen Victoria! He was then suddenly alarmed because I could see him – he faded away.

The strangest experience I had in that part of London was when walking close to Marble Arch. Suddenly I heard the roar of a huge crowd, and there before me I saw the most forlorn-looking man in a cart, with his hands tied behind his back. I glanced in the direction he was heading and, over the bobbing head of the skinny nag pulling the cart, I saw a hangman standing on a gallows! Suddenly the scene reverted to normal, and I had to leap to one side to avoid a number 8 bus going hell for leather.

It has been quite some time in London since the last public hanging held out in the open, where the well-to-do brought along picnic lunches to watch the event. But now instead there is Speakers Corner where people hang themselves by what comes out of their mouths!

After returning from Germany I spent some time working for Reuters in the sales division, and then moved on to the sales division of that huge company, Westinghouse. But after a while I was in search of more travel and education, so I went back to the Continent for a year. I spent time doing amateur readings, travelling, exploring different cultures, and discovering where my place in the world was destined to be and what I could do for a living that would be truly satisfying.

Eventually, I ran out of money and returned to look for another job, applying for one as a restaurant manager. I bluffed my way into this, and ran the restaurant extremely well for a year. Eventually I found another job that suited me, and that was once again in sales – selling telephone-answering machines. I did very well there and became General Sales Manager, but after a while I tired of the rat race.

I had used my psychic skills to great advantage in my selling, in my handling of staff, and in the day-to-day affairs of business. One example was when a young man applied for a job. He had no previous experience at all, but something told me to employ him. Everyone else in the management team was totally against this, but within one year the young man had sold more stock than any other top salesman in the previous five years! He went at his job hammer and tongs and left with a good stash of money – and me with a good reputation for picking the right people.

Yet all through this, I was becoming extremely dissatisfied with my situation. It was going more and more against the grain with me, and I was forced into making a decision by being literally shaken up. I had a car accident, and although I was not hurt I was jarred into thinking more deeply about my life. What happened was that I collided head-on with a taxi. The taxi driver flew out through his door, I went out through the windscreen, and once again the parade of my past went by. But then it stopped just at the point where the accident was occurring. I prayed, and then it moved on, but what came next was indistinct and blurry . . . The taxi driver was also unhurt, but the cars were slightly damaged. I felt somehow I had been given one last chance to fulfil my true destiny, so out into the world I went once again, in order to discover it . . .

I knew I had to have time to think, to retreat from the world for a while, so I went to Dunlaoghaire in Ireland, away from the hustle and bustle. Back to the home of my mother's ancestors. Dunlaoghaire was a relaxed and quiet town, about half an hour's drive from Dublin.

Typically, and without realizing it, I picked the most expensive part of Dunlaoghaire to live in. Every house other than mine seemed to be a millionaire's. Was it the shape of things to come? I was not a millionaire but I was comfortable, and I had enough to live well in Dunlaoghaire for a year. However, Eire is an expensive country. During that year I spent well over twenty thousand pounds, a lot to pay in order to liberate the soul and heal the body.

The peace and the general intelligence of local people I met amazed me. They were highly intuitive. The Irish clergy amused me terribly, and if ever I had a final and absolute reason for rejecting Roman Catholicism, then I am afraid those priests gave it to me. They did rule the people with a heavy hand. Many of the priests were sincere people, but they had a very conservative attitude, one that still hung on to the values of the Middle Ages.

My money began to run out. The need to be financially secure prompted me to return to the shores of Merrie Olde England, but the thought of going back to the world of sales sickened me. It was just far too superficial for me to consider.

I lived with a friend in her flat in Maida Vale. Rosie had an amazing son called George. By the time I knew him, he was seven years old and full of enthusiasm and common sense. Rosie suggested that to make a living I should use my psychometry and clairvoyance in order to change my situation. I was not very confident about doing it professionally, and I was unsure if people would be interested in coming to see me, but after a lot of thought I decided to give it a go. But before I went any further, suggested George, my name had to change – not my first name, but my surname. It was not catchy enough. At first I laughed, thinking the idea absurd, but the more I thought about it, this infant genius George was absolutely right! Rosie and I racked our brains. In the meantime, George had come up with another bright suggestion. He remarked that Peters and Lee, the singing duo, were a household name, so why not call myself Peter Lee. George felt this name would click with the public, and he was absolutely right. From the mouths of babes, as the saying goes. Then I thought that I should place an ad in a magazine and see what response I got.

I began my practice from a flat in Warwick Avenue, and then moved on about six months later. I continued my work in various places, and to my utter amazement soon found I was in demand. The work just came and came and came, until I could work no longer. I was totally and utterly psychically exhausted. So once again I took a break from the psychic world, and for a year applied my talents to the tourist business. I worked as a tour guide for German visitors, escorting them around Britain. During this time I discovered that I had been giving too much of myself in the process of my readings, so I learnt how to control my energy and not become over-tired. Even today, however, I am often left totally wiped out after heavy sessions involving great problems. Working as a tour guide was great fun, but inevitably the readings started again, as did the demand for them, so I started working a full hundred per cent, this time totally committed to what I now knew to be my life work. I had found my destiny, and I was in my late twenties then.

I had an office in Fleet Lane for a few months, near the Old Bailey, and later I moved to Noel Street in Soho for nearly two years, where I was inundated with clients, from kings and celebrities, politicians and pest controllers, to milkmen and funeral directors. Once again, by the time I'd finished working out of Noel Street, I was almost a nervous wreck, so I travelled to Munich to see friends, then to Paris and on to New York, returning at my leisure.

I found, to my surprise, I was able to re-establish myself extremely quickly. Over the years, I have always been extremely fortunate in having the boost of the press and media at large, helping to spread and enhance my reputation even more – through magazine interviews, radio chat shows and such. This in turn has helped to create a greater general interest in all things psychic and in my work, thus enabling me to reach a greater cross-section of the public.

Working as a professional clairvoyant altered my whole lifestyle, and eventually brought me into close and intimate contact with some of the truly great and interesting people of the twentieth century – the rich, powerful, artistic, infamous and tragic.

When I first started to work it was by trial and error. For a new psychic, I was in demand quite a lot. Sometimes I would get five clients in a day, but then five in a week. Within two months of wondering where the next pound was going to come from, I was booked up Monday to Saturday on a regular basis. I had a *living* wage. At that time, I was only charging four pounds a reading, but money was different then. Looking back, that amount seems terribly paltry compared to the fees charged by most psychics today, if they are any good. In those days I really flogged my guts out. But I soon learnt just how much I was worth. The artisan must charge for his labour, and at a price that does not devalue his work. Many people make it a bone of contention that psychics charge for their services, but in the world today money is the pole by which things are measured.

Like everyone else, a psychic has to eat, and have adequate surroundings in which to live and work. Those who charge and are genuine and good survive. Those who are genuine but cannot deliver the goods end up working as amateurs; those who are fakes will in the end be caught out. The psychic energies that move through a clairvoyant are demanding and tough. The fakes, from what I have observed, always eventually have nasty twists of fate. Bad things happen to them.

On several occasions, in the early days of my career, I was invited to do public demonstrations. One of the most interesting I did was for the Langian Society. There I was on stage, doing a cross between Shirley Bassey and Martin Luther King, telling people about their futures, their pasts, their hopes, dreams, problems and imaginings. I was giving them little psychic tasters that would help them to understand more about themselves. That audience was very responsive. As I came to the end of the demonstration, I sensed a young woman in the audience who seemed to be in a very negative and confused state. Her soul was desperately crying out for help.

At first it was difficult for me to speak to her, for I had to do so in such a way that others in the audience would have no idea at all of her identity. It was obvious this young lady did not want any attention drawn towards her. Yet she pleaded with me silently to help her. She had a secret – an awful secret – to hide.

My divination for her proceeded along these lines, for it was a chilling and highly complex situation.

'I see that you're trapped by a great, negative energy which is causing you considerable emotional pain. Yes, real misery. You can overcome it. You do realize that, don't you?' As my words sank in, she smiled a wistful smile of acknowledgement, sitting at the back.

I continued: 'It seems a self-elected state, my dear, that has taken control of you. It is most complicated and is definitely connected with the people you've sought out to play this nonsense with.' She certainly understood my meaning. But my time was up. The demonstration was over.

As the audience filed out of the hall, the pretty young girl, with long dark hair, beautiful skin and deep green eyes, approached me for further help. I continued speaking to her for about twenty minutes, in the hope of helping her to overcome the insidious burden she carried. She was only nineteen, and terribly insecure. She wanted to be good at something through which she could gain recognition – but had involved herself in an evil and twisted coven of witches. This witchcraft had nothing to do with the gentle, nature-loving religion that good witchcraft really is. As we talked, she began to cry, and deep inner tension began to be released. She was ready to recognize the pain that she was in, and asked me what to do.

'You have to seek a cleansing of some sort, something that will help you become balanced and happy again.'

As my words hung in the air, she mulled them over. She was relieved that at last there was someone whom she could consult about her problem. People belonging to that coven had been influencing her against her will with evil mental forces. I recommended that she should have no more contact with them in any way.

Like many other insecure people – young or old – she had taken what could be described as a shortcut to self-delusion.

The poor girl had become the product of the coven's selfish desires and had been *used* in many different ways, and in many revolting and weird rituals. However, she overcame these negative influences, and triumphed over the people who had caused them. She met a young man, fell in love and became happily and securely married. The weird people who had harmed her lost their hold and, from what I heard on the grapevine, the natural law of the universe considerably repaid them for their actions – which is often the way things work.

In the early days, as even now, fate pushed me into all types of circumstances where I was forced to use my abilities. Wherever I went, the psychic world was pressing in on me like a lovesick teenager. One of the personal hardships of a psychic as constantly busy as I am is the difficulty of establishing a meaningful personal relationship with someone who will be understanding, patient and loving. A psychic's skills belong to everyone, not to just one person exclusively. Because a genuine psychic is primarily a servant to his fellow human beings, he or she needs someone who is prepared to love when there is time to love.

Personally I feel that humanity, as a species, was generally made to experience many personal relationships in one lifetime. But there are, of course, those rare few who, for some deep and special reason, are destined to share their lives only with each other.

The two most important relationships I enjoyed were very different – highly entertaining and very, very moving.

One was with Susan, a true rose from Texas, and the other was with Andy, a very intriguing young man. They were both fulfilling relationships while they lasted, and from them I learnt a great deal about myself and other people.

I lived with Susan for three highly explosive years. She was used to having lots of money, and came from a very rich oil background. Sometimes she would throw the most incredible temper tantrums that I had ever witnessed. It was just like the onslaught of a hurricane. I think she had trouble in adjusting from one very luxurious lifestyle to another less flamboyant one. Her soft sensual accent, her exciting body with its curves in all the right places, and her complex personality completely won me over.

My relationship with her was passionate, violent, and never dull. Her temper, she said, came from her father. She was not very close to her family, and that caused her a lot of tension and insecurity. She used to fly into rages over the slightest things. I had an old bed, with big brass bed-ends, ideal for making love. So when we got into full swing, the bedsprings would start to squeak! The faster we went the louder squeaked the springs. I have always felt that love has its own music. Well, eventually, tantrum after tantrum, and good times after bad, we parted company through a terrible argument that could have come straight out of a silent movie from the early twenties. I can remember throwing a plate of bangers and mash at her, after incredible provocation. It missed her and decorated the wall just above her head. Then the plate fell on to her head. Sausages and potatoes adorned her hair. Unforgivably, I just laughed.

Faster than any of the Texas Rangers, she hurled a jar of tomato sauce and a couple of soft-boiled eggs. They hit me right in the face. I stood there fuming as she packed her bags and left. I wished her well before she got into the taxi and drove away into the vastness of metropolitan London. I never saw her again. Perhaps she is now home on the range.

I then lived with Andy, whom I nicknamed Randy. I thought this was highly amusing, but he was terribly embarrassed by it. In some ways he was quite shy, but he was also very attractive, with a young muscular body and a highly developed wit. We were together for two years. Sexually it was very good, but in many ways it was a time of anguish for me. He was always doing stupid and irresponsible things, and forever getting himself into debt, which I found totally idiotic. Eventually the final countdown came. After trying to sort things out and giving him many chances to improve himself, I had to make him pack his bags and go, for I could not waste my life running after him. Sad but true, this is a lesson that many of us learn when we fall in love: you cannot let loved ones drag you down. Relationships can be of immense value in helping to discover your true identity, for never should anyone have to compromise himself to make someone else happy.

Essentially, I am a psychic serving the designs of higher forces in the aid of humanity. So now relationships become less and less important as I grow closer and closer to my spirit and its vibrant link with the universal light of creation.

Chapter 5
Stranger than Fiction

My time spent working as a clairvoyant is never dull, I can tell you. Excitement, surprise and challenge are the norm in everyday routine. I never know from one moment to the next what bizarre situation is going to leap out at me with fangs ready for the kill. Having a sense of humour makes it much easier to relieve the tension that my calling brings, and I believe that when anything weird or mysterious does happen, it serves to test my character enormously, and thus strengthen my psychic abilities.

Nearly everyone comes to me for the same basic reason: for confirmation or assurance that their plans and hopes will work out well. Of course there are also people who come to me in desperation, seeking advice and guidance on problems that confuse them, or in situations where they can see no way out. But for every problem there is an answer. In many ways, I regard this aspect of my work as the most fulfilling. Many people have the mistaken impression that I am a medium – I am *not*! I am a clairvoyant. The distinction is a vitally important one. Mediums are people who are able to contact and speak with the dead. The clairvoyant is someone who uses a highly advanced form of ESP to uncover the mysteries of the past, present and future for a client. A clairvoyant can foretell or predict what will really take place. I, like any good clairvoyant, can see the destiny of each person who comes to me for guidance. I often steer clear of mediums, many of whom are, on the whole, frauds. Of course there are a few genuine ones, but to be a genuine medium is very rare indeed.

In my earlier days of psychic development I did have a tendency towards mediumship, but it did not interest me in the same challenging way as clairvoyance or prediction.

Seership, or the ability to predict accurately, seemed to me to be far more useful for a client's sake than mediumship. And, as I was able to refine my abilities, mediumship dropped away and I found that I had discovered my real talents.

Whatever you would like to call me – a soothsayer, a twentieth-century seer, or a cosmopolitan fortune-teller – you would be absolutely right. My gift is all things to all people. The saying 'Truth is stranger than fiction' certainly applies in my case. As I said earlier, I get a great cross-section of people consulting me, and as a result some of my clients are people whom you could only describe as on the lunatic fringe. There was a time in my career when I had nearly everyone famous that you could think of coming to see me, from Antony and Cleopatra – who happened to share the same personality – to Julius Caesar, as well as Mark Antony again! Both of them must have been looking for Cleopatra. What would happen if Mark Antony met himself? There was Joan of Arc, who came twice, but secretly disguised as different people, Lord Nelson, Elvis Presley, a number of Christs, two Buddhas, one Mohammed and a couple of Virgin Marys. Also one very thin man who thought he was the reincarnation of Sir Winston Churchill, but he hated smoking and this caused serious problems for him! Far more sinister, I had someone who thought he was Jack the Ripper, as well as one really weird situation – the client claimed that he was me!

I am a great believer in my full eight hours, when I can get it, but often sleep is a luxury to me. At three in the morning, my door was pounded so loudly that I thought the hinges would pop and the lock would snap in two. It seemed all hell had broken loose and was running around the streets of Chelsea. Half-dazed with sleep, half-crazed from the shock, and extremely annoyed, I stumbled to the door, assuming something terrible had happened to one of my friends. As I opened the door, a huge, overpowering man, resembling Quasimodo on a bad night, barged his way into my apartment and fell grovelling at my feet. Any moment I expected to hear a church bell toll! I thought to myself this must all be a bad dream. It was not really happening, was it? It was stress; I was working too hard, that is what it was. But it was not . . .

I motioned him to rise, feeling like the king of the beggars, and as he got up, he kept on growing and growing. I wondered how far the telephone was from my reach. Desperate thoughts rushed through my mind. Was he a thief? A reporter? A rapist? What? He stared at me for what felt like five minutes before saying anything. I became even more nervous. He cleared his throat with a harsh cough and then told me that he had hitch-hiked all the way from Newcastle-upon-Tyne, hundreds of miles, to see me. But why at three in the morning? This thought reverberated through my sleep-deprived mind. He went on to tell me that he was a merchant seaman (I hoped he was not going to show me his tattoos), and he claimed he had been commanded to come and see me by his voices. They had informed him that I, without a stain of doubt, was in fact Jesus Christ!

At this point, I grew very impatient. The gall of the man to come here and bother me with this! I wondered how I could get rid of him without being ripped into little pieces. He looked as if he bent anchors into shape for a living. He went on to inform me that I was the Chosen One destined to lead him to his mystical master in Tibet. He wanted to know if we could start immediately. He had the money for the travel tickets, and everything else.

I explained to him patiently that I did not know anything about all this, and that I certainly was not Christ, and he should put his money into a bank. He seemed rather annoyed. My five feet eight inches did not seem to measure up to his six feet nine of solid muscle, and he looked as though he weighed at least eighteen stone.

'Why pick on me?' I thought. 'There's plenty of people who claim they're Christ. Why can't he go and see one of them!' I just wanted to go back to bed. He then asked me to confirm the fact that he was St Paul . . .

Several exasperating hours later I managed to convince this poor man that he was indeed on a false errand. Finally he left, walking out into a wet, misty day in frantic search of his Chosen One. Perhaps he had read too many Lobsang Rampa books. He told me that he had sent a telegram warning me of his arrival, and sure enough the Post Office, living up to its reputation for reliability, delivered it two days later.

Unfortunately there are all too many people caught up in such tragic self-delusion, and the role of any caring psychic is to do as I did; with the aid of my clairvoyance I pointed out the sad error of his ways.

*

I once had a very faithful and extremely serious Alsatian dog, called Bonce because of the size of his head. This was quite large, and he kept knocking it, when he was a puppy, against doors and chairs. Bonce used to sit near me during readings. He was a very gentle dog and he had a marked sense of humour. So, like a canine butler, he would meet clientts at the door and escort them to their seats; and, once everything was to his satisfaction, the reading would begin.

A long-standing client introduced me to a friend of his, a lady from Australia who was very eager for a reading. When they arrived, Bonce went through his usual little ritual. The lady entered the consulting room, while her friend waited in the reception area. However, she was totally unprepared or misinformed as to what I did, for the result was indeed strange. I did her reading. She paid me and seemed very satisfied with what I had told her. Then she and her friend went off on their merry way. I thought nothing more of it, and went on to my next client, a Japanese pearl-diver.

The following afternoon I received a very curious phone-call from the client who had referred her to me. Utterly amazed, I listened . . .

As they were driving home, my client asked his Australian friend, 'Well, what did you think of the reading Peter gave you?'

At first there was no reply, then: 'Oh, he was quite good, actually. Yes, quite good!' She was from Queensland, where people are straight to the point, and she continued, 'He's a bloody fake, though! A good con man, but a bloody fake!'

My client was absolutely shocked – and so was I when I heard.

'A fake! How do you mean? Explain yourself!' he demanded. The woman merely sighed.

My client continued, 'I've always found Peter extremely accurate and very honest. I don't understand what you mean at all.'

'He just is, that's all.'

'Was he accurate about your past?' queried my client.

'Yes, he was absolutely accurate. He was good, hit the spot right on the nose. As a matter of fact he's probably right about the future.'

'Well, then, what's your problem?'

'I distinctly saw the dog sending him signals!' whispered the woman. My client couldn't believe his ears. The woman continued. 'The dog's lips moved. The dog was the psychic, you know – he was just picking up the signals from the dog!'

Some months later, after a refreshing dose of normality, seeing ordinary people with genuine problems and putting my gifts to real use, I received a strange telephone call from a lady who lived near Oxford Street in London. She asked me how much I would charge if I came to see her at home. I inquired why she could not come to visit me at my office. Her health seemed all right, but she insisted that I come to her. For the hell of it, I quoted an exorbitant fee, and to my surprise she accepted. The next day I took a taxi, which I charged to her. When I arrived at her front door, I was greeted by a shy and mousy-looking housekeeper. Then I was greeted by an enormous lady in a highly-revealing lilac nightdress which disclosed, amongst other things, a pair of shocking-pink suspenders! Had I come to the right house? What had I let myself in for? Kinky sex in the inner sanctum of the medical profession? This woman looked strong enough to go fifteen rounds with any world champion heavyweight boxer.

We entered a sitting-room with wonderfully high ceilings and large arched windows. The walls were an uncomfortable orange, the curtains a shocking pink, the carpet was dark brown, and there were large sofas in an orange floral pattern. It was so revolting it made my head swim.

Paintings buyable from a major department store for under five pounds dominated the walls rather than decorated them, and bad imitations of Michelangelo's statue of David adorned either side of the fireplace. Fluffy toys sat cutely on the edge of red velvet cushions in the middle of the sofas, three in all. The atmosphere was, at best, entertaining. The room stank with stale cigar-smoke and ashtrays were piled with cigarette butts, except one, in which she had deposited the remains of a chicken dinner. She yelled for the house-keeper, who rushed in to clear away this unseemly mess. The housekeeper gave me a weird smile, as if she was in the know about something that I was not. Clearly the lady was already half drunk, and she finished half a bottle of vodka before I was able to start the reading – and set her housekeeper the task of getting more. She drank most of another bottle during our encounter.

Her reading revealed much pain due to great suffering. It came out that she was, unbelievably, a high-class hooker – perhaps for those men who like a game of rugby or Olympic wrestling thrown in with their sexual pleasures, or maybe a bit of S/M. But what she did for a living did not worry me: everyone has the right to make a living in the way they see fit. This unhappy, tormented woman went in fear of her children discovering what she did for a living. It was in order to provide a good education and financial security that she did what she did – so that she could improve the lives of her children. It was the only way she knew how, and it was destroying her; but her children's welfare came first. As the reading came to an end, for which in some ways I was grateful, I made to leave.

Suddenly and to my utter amazement, with parts of her nightdress falling open and the bareness of her ample body all too evident, she expertly grabbed me and locked me into full nelson! She then flipped me over and spun me round, and I found myself with my head clasped between her thighs, lying on the floor and looking up into her crazed face. Why the hell did I ever come here, I wondered, and if I bit her leg would she let me go – or pummel me into the floor?

She then demanded that I tell her the 'truth'. 'You're him, aren't you! . . . Yes, I can see it in your eyes!' Relaxing her thighs a little, she bent over me, covering my face with her large breasts. I did not know whether to laugh or cry.

'What do you mean?' I pleaded pitifully.

She hesitated for a moment, her rage and grip subsiding, and in a very gentle voice said '*Jesus.*'

Not again – the thought raced through me. Were the lunatics of England planning a Peter Lee Persecution Year?

'*No, I'm not!*' I said, as forcefully as I could in the circumstances.

'You are. Why don't you just admit it. Come on, tell me!' Suddenly she let me go.

I stood up, rather shaken. There before me stood this huge woman, almost naked except for the pink suspenders and stockings. She said quietly, 'You're not leaving here until you tell me the truth.'

I sighed. I'd had enough of this fiasco.

'You can tell me, you know. *She* was here!'

'Who was here?' I implored.

'Why, the Blessed Virgin Mary.' Then this woman

mentioned the name of a well-known woman psychic who had clearly suffered a similar fate to my own. If this was going to become an occupational hazard, I thought, I might as well become a bank clerk!

Then she proceeded to offer me huge amounts of money if I would reveal the 'truth'. But, getting nowhere, she moved on to a time-honoured method of persuasion – if I did not tell her this 'truth' she would mash me up into little pieces. Then, before I could reply, she screamed, 'Who am *I* then? Go on, tell me. Yes, that's right: I am St Bernadette! That's how I knew you were him, the Messiah!'

Completely agreeing with her, I ran out of her apartment as fast as I could and hailed a taxi. On arriving home safe but breathless, I relaxed with a quiet drink, thinking just how close I had come to being a martyr to the woman's madness. She was terrifying in her menace.

London must have the largest collection of latter-day saints and modern messiahs of any city in the world! But at least this St Bernadette shared her favours and gave alms, even if for a price. I prayed that her voracious drinking would subside and that peace would come to her. As I prayed I knew in my heart that this prayer would be answered. The woman's situation has to be viewed with deep understanding and generous compassion. She was trapped by her profession, and I knew by my clairvoyance that deep down within herself she felt guilty for the way she made a living. She was truly tragic. In some respects her violence towards me was a misguided plea for help . . . but I could not really give her the kind of help and assurance she needed.

Many people come to me out of sheer curiosity, eager

to experience the psychic first-hand. Or they will try ever so stupidly to discredit it. One of the funniest and most innocent of these situations was when I tried to do a reading for a very amiable Scotsman. The telephone rang.

'Hello, is that Peter Lee, the psychic fellow?'

'Yes, I am Peter Lee, would you like to make an appointment?'

'Yes, I'd like to make an appointment, but, eh, well, eh, I don't really believe in all this, you know, but I'm a wee mite curious, and to be on the safe side, just in case, I'm bound to give it a go. I've heard you're the best!'

The man spoke in such a strong Scottish accent that he could turn milk into butter by just talking to it! Anyway, the day for his appointment came and he arrived on time, and was slightly nervous. He was very well dressed.

As I showed him into the consulting room, I said: 'Tell me, what part of Scotland do you come from? It's a beautiful country.'

The man stopped dead in his tracks. He stared at me with total surprise. 'My God! Christ Almighty! How the hell did you know that I came from Scotland!'

Before I had a chance to explain, he said firmly, 'It must be true! It must be true!' I could not stop him from giving me the money. He placed it on the table in a flash and left, yelling, 'It's true, it's true. Just wait until I tell Kirsty McBride!'

I never saw him again. I tried to find him in order to send the money back! In the end I accepted it as a gift from the gods. In his honour, I bought a good bottle of genuine heavenly nectar: Scotch whisky!

*

My career has placed me in some very highly-charged situations, but two of the most unexpected concerning what I term 'spontaneous mediumship' took place without any warning. They stick in my mind because they were an indication of just how strong the spirit world can be when there is a real need to communicate something of importance.

I had been helping two German ladies, and surprisingly their situations were very similar. One of the ladies, who was highly distraught and quite confused, had travelled all the way to Great Britain just in the hope of seeing a medium who might help her come to terms with her problem.

A good friend of mine was visiting the headquarters of the Spiritualist Association of Great Britain. Just as she was about to leave, she came across a very upset woman crying in the hallway. My friend, becoming concerned, asked her what was wrong. The woman replied, in German, that none of the mediums could help her because of the language barrier. It was certainly good fortune that my friend could speak German. After she had listened to this lady's unhappy story, she told her about me, and telephoned to see if I could help. I said I would see her, but only for a general reading, and it must be made very clear that I could not be regarded as a proper medium in any way at all.

Within the hour, the lady was at my door. We chatted away, mainly small-talk in German, until she felt reasonably composed.

As soon as I began the reading I started to feel strong and intense psychic forces trying to contact me, and, with this lady's despair so obvious, something told me to concentrate just on her, and there before me came the face of a very handsome young man of about fifteen or sixteen. He had corn-coloured hair, a bright, happy, golden yellow. His skin was milky, and he was rosy-cheeked. His eyes were a clear blue, but he looked as though he was shocked.

As I described this boy, she called out his name – it was her son talking to her from beyond the grave! He called her 'Mother' and her tears came in torrents. She began to laugh and cry at the same time. The son gave his mother a consoling message, proving that love spans even death. Apparently her son had died in a climbing accident only the year before. Slowly the message from her son faded, as if a wind was blowing the sound of his voice away. I myself felt overcome with the intensity of the situation, and was quiet for a while, so as to let the dead son's words sink in. She was astonished that at last she had been able to speak to him. How she had missed him! I then felt the presence of another spirit personality, this time older and far more serious. This spirit identified himself as the woman's husband – it turned out that he had died in the same climbing accident. Once again this message was full of comfort and reassurance; and then her husband told her she should marry again – preferably the man she had just met.

She began to laugh with real joy. The weight of guilt and worry slipped off her shoulders. She told me that she had a special feeling for a man she had recently met, and he had asked her to marry him. But she had been unsure, for she was in love with her departed husband. What I had told her related to the crux of the problem. She went back to Germany a very happy woman, and six months later she was married, secure in the blessing of her departed loved ones.

For many hours after that reading, my consulting room was charged with the energy of love and joy from that harmonious union of the spirit and material worlds.

*

The other occurrence of spontaneous mediumship took place in the bustling city of Munich when I was on a guest tour of Germany. Once again, a woman was racked with despair. The second I sat down with her, the power of a stronger force flowed through me. I saw that her despair was contorting her very personality, and that she was cruelly imprisoned by her doubts about her only son's death.

As I concentrated upon her situation, I experienced her confusion, her searching for the truth, and at that point, the words just rolled off my tongue: 'I have a message for you, from your son!' Both of us were shocked at the words. Even though I speak fluent German, I asked her if she understood what I said, because at first I did not believe it. Before me came the image of her son. He was covered as though by a deep mist of depression. Suddenly a large number of voices began trying to talk to me – but I concentrated just on the son and the others subsided. Soon I was able to relate the message from son to mother.

'Mother, it's very important that you listen to me. Yes, Mother, I am dead, but you just have to accept that I didn't commit suicide, as you were led to believe. I died from an overdose of drugs, Mother, an overdose . . . I was scared, but everything is getting better now, so don't worry.'

As I related this message, the boy's mother listened dumbstruck. She had discovered at last the truth about her son's death. There was more, but I cannot speak about it, for it was confidential. The woman sat with her mouth open in astonishment, gazing at me imploringly. I knew what she was thinking, so I said as gently as I could, 'No, I can't bring him back, and he'll only return to the material world when he is ready. He is much better off where he is now. Please be assured of that, and you will help him on his way.'

The woman smiled at these words, for the truth of them made a deep impact within her heart. She left me, transformed. Years of pain and doubt had been washed away; for the first time in five years she could think of her son without grief. She now knew that he was safe.

I have come to the opinion that those in the spirit world will always force their way through if the need is great enough. Seldom do they want to deal in the affairs of this world, but if there is no choice they will. On the whole, a lot of supposed contact with the spirit world is, I fear, pure imagination, and is often of no real help to anyone.

People now in the spirit world are often attributed with knowing more than they really do. Most times, they remember their earth life as if it was a dream. They have a very *different* understanding of reality, except for those who have just arrived there, and it must be stated that, just like people on earth, they too have their failings and are equally trapped by their desires, by time and space. It is necessary to remember that a spirit cannot always be of any real help to us. The only spirit that can be truly helpful is your higher self – your own inner psychic abilities.

In fact, I feel that the spirit world is purely an extension of this life – as this life is an extension of the spirit world. It consists of many planes or marked points of progress, and I know that the world we live in is in fact one of the lower points in the various planes of reality. We are sent here, or come here, to cope with certain experiences that we must learn. Thus someone as psychically sensitive as myself has come here in order to learn how to serve my fellow human beings.

Amid this serious talk of spirits and the spirit world there is always room for humour. One funny incident that happened to me is a perfect example of how people overreact to the psychic world, or read far too much into anything slightly associated with it. This situation occurred quite recently. A lady came to see me for a reading, and kept insisting that everything I told her was in fact messages coming directly from her grandfather, who had recently died. The harder I tried to convince her that this was not the case, the more she insisted that her grandfather wanted to contact her via me. I told her repeatedly that I was not a medium, but she didn't believe me.

My two cats are very cheeky animals. Trotsky, the fat ginger tom, is full of cunning and subtle mischief and sits on people whether they like it or not. Chow-Chow, the svelte Russian Blue, is probably influenced by watching too much television, for she takes on various character roles for every minute in the day. She has a tendency also to climb up the curtains and jump down on top of unsuspecting clients. So when these two rascals get locked out of my consulting rooms they normally make a huge fuss by rattling the french windows.

Just as I was coming to the most important part of the reading – the climax – the doors to the consulting room began to shake violently, and, as the glass in them is mirrored, my client could not see what was causing this. Possessed by this bizarre situation, she stood up with arms raised outwards and yelled, 'Grandfather, at last it's you. You have returned!'

At this point the doors began to swing open. The woman, almost hysterical, screamed and fainted on to the floor. Pure Hollywood drama!

The cats peeked timidly into the room. They stalked

around as if nothing had happened, then fell asleep in their chair. When the woman came to, she felt all right, but was upset that she had missed the vision of her grandfather – so close to the supernatural but yet so far away.

On a more personal note, I did a reading for an old friend of mine that shook me to my very core. George Hoft was also a famous inventor (one of his many claims to fame was the bullet-proof vest and jacket used extensively by the American police), an author, a bouncer, a taxi driver, and many other things. He was divorced, but had a family and a mistress – in other words, he was a man who had lived his life to the full. During World War II he was a child prisoner of the Japanese in Indonesia. In fact, he was half Indonesian and half Dutch, which in itself gave him an unusual perspective on the world.

When George came to me for a reading he was desperate. Something did not feel right. He was edgy, uneasy, as if something was going to happen – something that he half knew or felt, but could not put his finger on. He just turned up on my doorstep demanding a reading, so we sat down and had a cup of coffee. When I asked how I could help him, George became a little more relaxed, and slowly I began to do a reading.

'George, I can see you going on a journey. This is a trip you have thought a great deal about. It is the most important one that you'll ever take. This is a journey that for some reason you've never had the chance to take, but soon – within a few days – you will. It will be the strangest journey that you've ever made.'

George gave me an odd look. I continued, unaware of the importance of what I was saying. 'You've done

99

it all, George. This journey will mean a completely new start for you.'

My words made him flinch. 'I know what you mean, Peter,' he said with a silent sureness.

From that point on, George diverted the reading to other subjects ... Three days later he was dead.

George knew he was going to die. I did not know or consciously realize that I had predicted his death. It was as if I was just a mouthpiece to help him prepare for the greatest journey anyone on this earth can ever make. On the morning of the funeral I was getting myself ready to go and pay my last respects, and, just as I was leaving, I felt George's presence and I psychically heard George's voice say to me, 'Peter, I'm not here any more. Don't come. There's no need.'

What George meant was that he was not at his funeral, or on earth. I decided not to go any further. I went back inside, changed my clothes, poured a drink and in silence dwelt upon my friendship with George. I found the tears welling up inside me, for I really missed the physical presence of a close and trusted friend.

Many of my other friends were very angered that I did not attend George's funeral. One eventually asked me why. At first I was lost for words, but then they came. 'Because,' I said, 'George wasn't there.' My friend, on the other end of the telephone, was quiet for a moment, and then soberly replied that he understood.

I often wonder why I was selected by fate as the one to tell him of his death.

The ability to heal is within all of us, for through all of us flows the creative life force of nature. Yes, the very energy that upholds nature moves through us, giving us life. It is this energy that can be used to heal other people, if we only learn how to tune in to it, direct it, and use it properly. The act of using the life force, or psychic energy, is in fact the merging of two minds and the exchange of willpower and trust. A good healer can create in his or her patient the desire to be healed. Once the patient has the desire to be healed, half the healing is done, because the power of the mind in the patient is liberated. This, of course, then allows the life force of the healer to do its work more effectively.

I would like to share a truly amazing incident of healing with you, where the higher forces of the spirit world came to my aid. I do not often do healing – only in cases of real need. This time I felt that I should apply my powers to heal a little child.

When I was working out of Rennie Court, which overlooks the Thames, I was doing a reading for a certain lady. I mentioned to her that she had two children – a boy and a girl. She said that was right, but there was a taint of sadness in her voice. Her little boy seemed to be locked in some type of mental prison where the outside world was like a nightmare from which he could not escape. The lady immediately burst into convulsive tears of grief, sobbing her heart out. Through her tears she forced out the words, 'Yes! My son is mentally handicapped!'

A great rush of psychic energy went through me. I said to her, 'I don't feel he is mentally handicapped in any way at all.' She said that doctors had told her that there was no chance for him to have a normal life like other little boys and he would never be able to read or hold intelligent conversations. 'He is *not* a vegetable! The doctors are wrong!' I said to her firmly. She smiled, and I continued, 'There is a very sweet and very intelligent soul behind this locked mind. I feel that if you would like to bring him to me, I can help to heal him.'

She looked at me in silence. Then she spoke. 'That's marvellous, Mr Lee. I am really amazed, because many years ago, just after my son was born, I went to see a gypsy fortune-teller. She was famous and very genuine. She said that one day I would go to see a great man who lived by a river, and if I took my son to him this man would heal him.' It was my turn to be amazed!

The little boy was brought to me on a number of occasions. After several intense healing sessions he was able to read normally, and he improved in just about every way. The psychic forces of nature and the universe healed this lovely child.

On one other occasion, I did healing for a client who was desperately ill and had pleaded with me to help him. This happened in the United States, and I was rather nervous about healing this man, because he was a lieutenant to the Don, or boss, of a major Mafia family. If I fail, I thought, I may be the one in need of healing! He was a very large, fat man, with a double-edged sense of humour. He suffered from strange expansions of his bodily tissues, his blood was diseased, and he was grossly overweight. He also had high blood pressure, but for all of this he was quite a relaxed man!

Fortunately, my healing worked. His problems subsided completely, and this high-ranking executive of crime was very pleased indeed with his new-found health and vigour. I know that he is still leading a perfectly normal life.

Psychic healing is all part of the psychic gift. It is part and parcel of the same energy which enables me to give readings. There are those who are born with the natural gift of healing in abundance, and because I am so busy predicting I recommend people to other healers. I do urge them to seek out good healers. They can alleviate pain and suffering, and the really good ones can actually effect cures. Many aches and pains and other problems cannot be healed by orthodox medicine, so this is where the psychic healer comes in. The psychic healer has been serving humankind since man first walked the earth.

Chapter 6
Star Predictions

One of the most inspiring people I have had the good
fortune to meet and get to know was the legendary
singer Bob Marley.

I was having a quiet drink at a well-known and
extremely fashionable hotel in Knightsbridge with a
close friend of mine, one of whose lesser claims to
fame is the elaborate and extremely well-orchestrated
practical jokes he likes to play.

There we were, my friend and I, at about three
o'clock in the afternoon. I had just finished work for
the day and was enjoying my well-earned break, when
out of nowhere a piercing hoot and a wild yell cut
through the quiet of the bar.

My friend's name was called, and I turned round to
see who had caused all this unseemly commotion. I
nearly tripped over myself, for there across the way
stood the exact double of Bob Marley. The man was a
dead ringer for him. Then I thought, 'Oh, my God!
Here we go. Another practical joke.' I braced myself
for the coming ordeal by ordering another Martini.

This duplicate Bob Marley casually sauntered over
to where we were, stopped and smiled a huge, generous
smile at my friend. Then he looked at me warmly as if
he had known me all his life. He had a mischievous
twinkle in his eyes that was quite contagious. This just
had to be another trick, so I remained impassive.

'Peter, I'd like to introduce you to a good friend of

mine I've known for years – Bob Marley. Bob, meet Peter Lee.' My friend's words did not convince me – this had to be another tedious prank. 'Now let's all have a friendly drink,' he continued.

'Why does he do this kind of thing?' I thought. I was not impressed. Megastars were not this casual! Where were the crowds wildly mobbing him? I could see no one straining for a touch of his dreadlocks. Where were the bodyguards?

The impostor turned to me and said, 'What's wrong, then? Don't you believe I'm Bob Marley?'

I looked at him and said, 'Yes, I'm sure you are, and I'm Elizabeth Taylor doing an impression of Moses!' The other two looked rather hurt.

Just at that point two huge men sauntered into the bar looking anxiously about.

'His bodyguards,' whispered my friend. Then through the bar window I saw a large gold Mercedes saloon pull up and one of the large men called out to the impostor, 'Mr Marley, we're ready to go when you are.' I was dumbstruck. Suddenly the truth knocked me sideways – 'He *is* Bob Marley! Oh my God, I must look like a real idiot!' But he laughed at my consternation and we had another drink.

Our chance meeting, obviously decreed by fate, brought us together subsequently a number of times, and as we got to know each other much better, Bob felt confident enough to ask if he could come over and see me for a reading. I got to know him best in the year before his death. For many great artists, life is short and very demanding. I did realize that he was going to die soon, and I know, as he humbly pointed out, I was instrumental in helping him accept the fact that he did not have long to live. I helped him come to terms with death and make provision for his wife and children, and their future security. Bob was a highly sensitive, often shy man. He had a great sense of spirituality about him, a gentle charismatic quality that enlivened everything he touched. He had a deep natural intuitive knowledge of the psychic world, and was in some ways psychic himself.

At the time when I was giving him readings, Bob was travelling a great deal between London, the West Indies and Ethiopia, searching deeper into his spiritual and cultural roots, for that was highly important to him.

It is a privilege to have known this great man. He was a true world leader, in a spiritual sense, for he was responsible for giving many people of different races a great deal of inspiration and hope. Regardless of what some people may think, he was a strong proponent of non-violence and responsibility: he always advocated peace and multi-racial harmony. Marley was small, almost fragile in stature, but gigantic and generous in spirit. I have no doubt at all that he was a prophet of sorts. In the readings that I did for him, his concern for the underprivileged of the world became apparent, and he helped many needy people, groups and individuals, in quiet inconspicuous ways.

The words of his songs were prophetic. They state important truths so simply that any listener can easily understand them. I feel his entire message can be summed up in his beautiful and haunting 'Redemption Song'.

My life will always be the richer for knowing him, laughing with him, sharing his sorrows, but most of all for the hope he held in his heart for his fellow human beings. All he wanted was for the world to be a better place.

*

Another man whom I can say wholeheartedly I was glad to encounter was Charlie Kray. Society in the United Kingdom may regard him as an arch-villain, a criminal, an anti-social person, a gangland boss. But he is not.

Charlie has often been unfairly tarred and feathered by the press. He is a highly complex person and a total gentleman. He has paid his dues to society many times over and is now an honest businessman. His past is far behind, and he is well removed from his former gangland associations. He has regularly come to me for consultations, and I regard him as perfectly genuine and open in all his dealings. He once succumbed to infamy through seeking out a better life than he had as a child. But during his time as Britain's number one gangster, he also did a great deal of good for people less fortunate than himself. He is the eldest of the Kray trio; and his two younger brothers are still in prison.

After Charlie's release from prison, he became, almost overnight, a cult figure. He also became an author, and developed financial interests in the recording and film industries. Charlie is a dapper dresser, combining style and flair with an old-world charm.

One of Charlie's long-term aims is to obtain the release of his two brothers from prison. They have paid long enough for their crimes. Psychically I feel that he will achieve the release of one of his brothers in coming years. Charlie himself lives a quiet life, enjoying the fruits of his labours gained through socially acceptable means.

Charlie Kray is not the only reformed character I have met. Some time ago I was visited by a gentleman who had come to me for a reading in a desperate state of mind. As he sat in front of me, it was psychically obvious that he was in acute depression, as if he had nothing more to live for. I realized that I had to find something to cheer him up, but unfortunately I had to tell him that I saw cold steel bars around him. I felt he was under tremendous pressure, and that he was in some serious legal trouble. I suggested he had been smuggling drugs and that he had been to prison and was now out on bail, and he confirmed all this was true. Then I told him that he was going to stand trial again, quite soon. This he also confirmed. Regretfully, I had to tell him he would spend three long years in prison because of his crimes.

He was very relieved when I told him this, for in that moment the troubled man made peace with himself and accepted that he would have to pay the price for breaking the law. He now knew there was no point in swimming against the tide.

He was sentenced for three years, but was paroled after eighteen months for excellent behaviour. He is now happily treading the straight and narrow, and is a totally changed person – much for the better. He has come back to me several times since. All my readings have proved absolutely accurate, and uplifting for him. I predicted his marriage to a lovely woman, and the two children they now have. By accepting justice he transformed himself.

Many people of all kinds come to me for advice, from the famous already established in their chosen careers to highly talented young people on their way up. One person who is most definitely on her way up the spiral staircase to fame, fortune and posterity is the stunningly beautiful Charlotte Lewis. She is fast becoming an international star of huge proportions. She is an exciting and alluring blend of sophistication, sensuality and a genuine child-like innocence. Charlotte is a close friend and completely natural, without any pretension. At eighteen, she was already a highly respected international model, and is one of the brightest starlets to emerge from Britain in a long time.

Petite and mentally alert, her physical presence in the movies is hypnotic. From the age of fourteen she established herself securely as an international model, but with her torrential success came a deep desire to find a new direction in life. Something that would creatively fulfil her and at the same time involve her modelling skills. Her career was greatly enhanced by the efforts of journalist David Lichfield, but nevertheless she would have still made it without his assistance.

Charlotte first came to see me for a reading at the recommendation of another client, a famous fashion photographer. From that first encounter a happy association has developed over a period of years. In one reading involved with her career, a great flood of information came to me from the psychic world.

'Charlotte, in a very short time I see cameras around you.'

She sighed, looking rather put out, and said, 'What, more modelling work, Peter?'

'No, it's not that, Charlotte. The cameras are movie cameras and there's lots of flashing lights, yes, lots of lights. I smell the sea, applause. Yes, people are clapping, and someone very important is in the background.'

She laughed.

'No, take this seriously, Charlotte. You are without a doubt on the way to becoming a major movie star; and the first step is not far away.' The words rang in my ears.

'Oh, Peter, now, stop pulling my leg.'

I reassured her that what I was saying was fated to

happen, and that she should be aware of every opportunity that came her way.

About three months later she went off to Paris to do some exclusive modelling work for a major fashion house, and while she was there she met a prominent French film star. Acting on a hunch, he introduced her to the famous film director, Roman Polanski, who was so impressed that he rushed her to a film test for the starring and only female role in his new movie, *Pirates*.

The producers were overwhelmed by her and sooner than she had ever thought possible, she was under the lens of one of the world's best cameramen, and the direction of one of the greatest directors.

When she came back to see me with tears of joy, I reminded her that the psychic world holds all the secrets of the future.

Since *Pirates*, Charlotte has moved from strength to strength and has now completed a prime role in a new movie co-starring with the fabulous Eddie Murphy!

At the time of that prediction Charlotte was far removed from the world of movies, and seemingly had as much chance of becoming a film star as I do of becoming the next Prime Minister of England! But you never know. Life is full of changes and surprise.

In 1982, I had my office in Noel Street, London, in that area of intrigue, romance, seedy passion and haven of excellent restaurants known as Soho. Noel Street, which runs between Regent Street and Wardour Street, has its own particular charm, and is very near the London Palladium, the 'Palace of the Stars'. Because the popular weekly magazine, *Ms London*, had conducted a survey of psychics in London and voted me number one, I was then inundated with clients. I was booked up months in advance and was seeing at least ten to twelve people a day, an hour at a time, seven days a week. I had a permanent secretary in the office, and I do not know what I would have done without her. Isobel held everything together with her patience, common sense and well-developed sense of diplomacy. Also her sense of humour cut through the tension and melted the aggression of difficult clients.

My office was up a flight of stairs and was very ordinary but, thanks to Isobel's sense of decor, it became quite a pleasant place to work in, with gentle colours and plenty of pot plants, as well as copious amounts of hot fresh coffee for clients waiting to have a reading.

At times the office became very hectic. One day, when I forced Isobel to take her lunch-hour off for once, I stayed in to man the telephones – and wondered how she ever managed to stay on top, for as soon as I put down one phone, the other would start ringing.

At last there was a lull in this storm. As I sat back to enjoy the peace and quiet, the door to the reception area was flung open with a dramatic flourish. There stood a very imposing figure of a man.

He stood still as if waiting to be recognized or even applauded. At that point in the day I was not interested. 'I'm sorry, sir. The office is closed for lunch.'

There was no reply. Perhaps he did not hear me. Lots of people tried to get me to do readings for them during my lunch break. It just was not on. In the doorway, clad in a black cowboy's outfit that looked as if bought from one of those shops in Soho selling 'erotic designer clothes', still hovered this strange man, glaring at me with such intensity. He wore a white neckerchief. With his eyes on fire, he looked like something out of *The Magnificent Seven*. Yes, it was none other than Yul *King and I* Brynner. I was rather surprised that I eventually recognized him, because I'm quite notorious for not knowing famous people when I meet them face to face.

But I decided to have some fun and pretend not to know who he was. He pulled himself to his full height and walked over to me. 'I have come for a consultation . . . I hear that you're the best in Europe.' I looked up and smiled. 'I have come for my reading!' he demanded. Using my psychic faculty, I looked into him to see if his request warranted giving up my much appreciated break to do a reading for him. His desire for a reading was genuine, but I replied, 'Come back after lunch and my secretary will make an appointment for you in about four months' time. All right?'

This did not seem to go down too well. 'I want my reading now!' he stormed.

'So do a lot of other people, but you'll just have to wait your turn like everybody else,' I said firmly.

My words seemed to make him angry. 'Do you know who I am?'

'The face is familiar . . . Stick a lollipop in your hand and say, "Who loves you, baby?" '

When I burst out laughing, he looked shocked for a moment, then he burst out laughing too. The entire situation was ridiculous.

I told him that because of the gravity of his problem I would do a reading there and then. He seemed amazed that I should know about problems before he actually told me!

I was still doing his reading by the time the next client arrived. His reading finished, Yul thanked me greatly. As I opened the door to show him out, the client almost burst at the seams, reacting as if all her erotic dreams had come true at once.

After hearing of Yul's tragic death, many of the things that came out in his reading came home to me. In some ways he was a man like Bob Marley (except for the hair) in that he did a lot of good for people behind the scenes by using his wealth and influence intelligently. I genuinely admired his acting skills. I felt that he took control of the characters that he played, with a kind of psychic understanding similar to that of a medium tuning in to a spirit-person, and by doing this he made all his roles vibrate with a wild electricity.

At one time I lived next door to the singer Marvin Gaye. After a time we got to know each other quite well. This was when I was living in Park West, and we spent time together in genial conversations about the world and our work, and indirectly the psychic side of life. Sometimes, I had urged him to be careful, otherwise he might fall into harm of some serious kind. I always wondered if the warning was heeded. Then he was murdered tragically by his father!

I met another musician in 1983 when I was asked to do some predictions by the huge appliance manufacturers, Russell Hobbs, for their important guests at a function they were holding.

It took place at the swish nightclub, the Roof Garden in Kensington, owned by Richard Branson, the millionaire founder of Virgin Records, Virgin Books, and, of course, the airline. I was sitting quietly in the corner reading for people when, without warning, the doors were flung open with a crash and in came Kenny Ball and his Jazzmen playing 'When The Saints Come Marching In'. What hope in hell did I have of working amid all this racket? But on I went. I did not get away until the small hours, around three in the morning. Leaving the main area of the club, I went into a dressing-room, and there I bumped into Kenny himself. We had a drink and a chat, and he said to me, 'This psychic lark, load of bull, is it, Peter? Bit of a con, eh?'

'Not with me, Kenny, not with me,' I replied.

'What? I'd better come along and have a basinful of it myself, then,' said Kenny with a smile. 'Will you give me a discount, Peter?'

'No, Kenny, no one gets a discount!' We both laughed.

Kenny Ball is a really nice man: his attitude to life is very open.

As I walked out into the street in the early morning, the sun was rising. As I looked at it, for some strange reason I prayed that other people would live to see the sun rise over the teeming city of London a thousand years from now. The Thames, as I crossed it on my way home, gleamed and sparkled, alive with the promise of a new day. The early morning chimes of Big Ben rang out over the still, quiet city. I felt glad and privileged to be alive on such a day.

I watched the clouds part, gather and part again as early morning winds blew the day into life. I arrived home, climbed into bed and felt as if the dawn had been a gift just for me. And with that beauty filling me, I fell asleep as the city began to wake.

As I am a servant to the higher forces that mould and direct the shape of history, I am often taken into situations where I come face to face with people who decide the future of the world. Why is it that they come to a psychic? It is because they know that what they do can only take place if it works into an overall scheme, pattern or plan. Often the world has to have bad and horrific things happen to it in order to pay the debts that we, humanity, have created. That is the process of natural law. Natural law governs everything that we do; even the gifts of a psychic such as myself work upon the energy-flows of the natural law that blends humanity into a larger universe. I see into the future due to the trends that emanate from the path of natural law, so in some respects I am a dispenser of psychic justice to those who feel the need to inquire. Thus on many occasions I have been consulted by ex-prime ministers who still have a say behind the doors of power, and by one still in office concerning matters of the gravest importance. The subjects range from personal affairs to affairs of state, political personalities and world events at large.

One client whom I am always happy to see at any time, due to her maturity and warmth of character, is Mrs Henry Ford II. She is world-wise in the best possible way and highly informed as to all that happens on the world scene. She is a constant source of strength to her husband, as he heads one of the world's greatest and most prestigious industries, the Ford Motor Company. She has consulted me many times and it is a great pleasure to guide one of the world's most influential women. She pays me a great compliment by asking me for psychic consultations.

These days I am still surprised to see someone famous sitting opposite me in my consulting rooms. From members of various royal families through to high-flying oil men, pop stars and politicians, priests, psychics and giants of industry, many famous and infamous have come to me for help. These people, whom you would least expect to be seen consulting someone like me, are the ones I find most eager to act on the advice that comes to them, through me, from the higher realms where everything is known.

Because of the popularity of the personalities who consult me, I am of interest to the media at large. Fabrications and wild statements pop up with obvious predictability and tedious regularity, alleging some very risqué things indeed! For instance, in the *Daily Mirror* I was announced to the world in startling headlines as 'PRINCESS MICHAEL'S SECRET PSYCHIC'. Three or four national newspapers gave considerable coverage to this story.

I was the unfortunate victim of many snatch photographs, in which I am totally sure they did not catch my best features. In the dead of night, when not even a psychic could predict what was going to happen, there came furtive telephone calls demanding 'the truth'.

One clever young reporter was determined to get a story and exclusive photograph. After clearly reading too many Spiderman cartoons, he climbed up to my balcony, on the second floor of an apartment building! I had great pleasure in slowly pulling the curtains closed as this poor chap fumbled with his camera. As his flash went off, illuminating his presence for the nosy neighbours across the road, he was the recipient of much rather basic vocal attention.

During this time, 'No comment' was my middle name and the most common phrase on my lips. I had said nothing at all to the newspapers.

Even a princess has the right to consult a psychic. My main concern is the protection and privacy of my clients, whoever they may be. Once I was followed for miles by a reporter when I was driving to the coast.

Perhaps he imagined I had a secret rendezvous there with Her Royal Highness.

During this carousel of gossip, a most courteous journalist from the *Sunday Mirror* asked if he could take me to dinner in order to 'discuss the situation'. After dinner, which was excellent, this journalist rattled off a list of about a dozen names; names that moved the world. It was a miniature *Who's Who*. As he finished reciting from his hard-won list, he placed it dramatically on the table, and in a voice resembling Orson Welles in *The Lady From Shanghai* he said, 'Well, Mr Lee, what do you think of that!'

'What do *you* think about that?' I replied. I felt like giving him a gold star for effort.

'How about a straight answer?'

To be congenial and because the reporter was proud of his momentary coup, I replied, 'Yes, about eight of those names on your list are my clients. But I'm not going to tell you who they are – not even for money. Go ahead and publish that list if you like and let the other four sue; I might sue you myself!'

The rest of the evening was still quite enjoyable. But someone had been very naughty, and I made it my business to find out who the culprit was – a snake in the grass was out wriggling around London.

One reporter even asked me bluntly over the phone if I was having an affair with Her Royal Highness. This senseless and provocative speculation I quickly crushed. After about four to six weeks the whole fiasco luckily faded. From time to time some story-hungry reporter from the yellow press still tries to stir it all up again, but it falls flat and goes no further.

Looking at the Princess, it is only too obvious that she is an extremely fine person with great strength of character and the moral fibre that she needs to occupy

117

her position in society. She is a stable example of motherhood and has coped admirably with the enormous strains and pressures that have come her way lately. This is no psychic prediction but is plain to everyone.

Chapter 7
Catastrophe

One of my most frightening psychic experiences occurred when I had just begun to relax after a day's work. It must have been about midnight. The evening was quiet and still. A shower of light rain began to splatter on the windows, and bring the trees outside to life. I stared at the flames of my fire. The cracking and hissing of wet logs gave peace to the room. The flames cast long, dancing shadows over the walls. The cats, Trotsky and Chow-Chow, came up to the fireside and started to purr and I began to hear, at first faintly, the sounds of gunfire and the voices of people yelling and cursing. Immediately before me, there formed an intricate vision: a picture of confusion and urgency. My psychic faculties had suddenly expanded, and what I witnessed really shocked me.

At first I was high amongst some trees, but then I was gently falling towards luxuriant undergrowth that seemed to be forest or bush. I found myself on a long path that had been etched into the earth over many years by hundreds of feet. I looked up at the night sky. The stars seemed different. I heard people somewhere close speaking a language that sounded African in origin. I then saw a man running down the path. There was a large crowd pursuing him. The mob was firing guns at him. A bullet whistled right past me. I saw Idi Amin run straight by me – and I realized that I was invisible to him. I was there astrally. Amin had a gun in his hand. His face was stained with blood. He stopped and hid behind a tree and started firing at the pursuing crowd. A few of them fell dead. I saw their souls rise up and depart. I realized then I really was in a jungle. The crowd was coming closer. Amin's face became distorted with fear and horror. Sheer blind panic overtook him. I was seeing into the dictator's soul!

I knew that then and there a military coup was rising up to overthrow Amin. I was witnessing it before it actually took place! The military coup, however, would not be good for Uganda. A regime far worse would take savage control. Bloodthirsty terror was now stalking the streets and plains of Uganda.

Suddenly I snapped out of it. Everything around me returned to normal. I saw two hours had elapsed, but it had felt like only five minutes.

The next morning I knew that I must ring the Ugandan High Commission and tell them what I predicted. I did not want to see anything even worse replace Amin's already vicious and callous rule. I felt sorry for the ordinary Ugandan people. What would become of them under a regime that could make Amin seem mild by comparison?

Sadly my warning was laughed at by the Commission. But ghastly violence and insane bloodshed took place within the three-week time limit that I had predicted. The rest is sad and bitter history.

As you know by now, I have experienced some strange psychic situations, but one of the most frightening was when I literally fought for my life in a battle with a psychic 'monster'. This monster actually tried to murder me.

It all happened once when I was on holiday in Germany, and a friend kindly let me stay in his house.

Let me tell you about this friend's house. It was a very old building on the outskirts of Munich, and was covered in great wreaths of climbing roses. When I arrived, the house was ablaze with deep crimsons and scarlets, and a most beautiful scent greeted me as I walked up the garden path to the front door. This gave me the impression that the house was alive, the writhing vines of climbing roses giving a strange unearthly quality to the building. Little did I realize just how right my first impressions were!

The house was built from dark granite, and grey stone peered through the abundant roses, occasionally giving a somewhat sombre touch to the colourful display. The house was squarely built and was completely detached, the nearest neighbour being about a kilometre away, in a country area where agriculture was the predominant activity.

The house gave off vibrations of great age. It was about three hundred years old, and had six rooms in all, but they were large and well lived in. The garden around it was a strange mixture of wild abandon and careful maintenance. I can remember that as I passed in through the front door, a cold shiver ran down my spine, as if someone had walked over my grave. I was very tired then, yet fortunately my clairvoyance was alert.

All that evening I felt that something was not right. There was a malevolence in the atmosphere, but I could not quite put my finger on it. I began to sense bizarre events that had happened in the building many years ago. I felt as though I was slipping through the very fabric of time itself, back into some situation of horrendous murder. It was dim and murky. I saw two shadows

121

in front of me. I realized that I was looking from the future back to the past. Then I saw the flash of a knife! A horrible scream – then the shuffling, scraping sound of someone dragging a dead body away.

I became very uncomfortable, yet sensed that my friend did not feel this force at all. Throughout the evening I felt as if someone or something was watching me from an invisible domain. When I went to bed, I tried to relax. But a great suffocating sense of evil and despair rushed over me like a chill wind. I then began to smell a most revolting stench. Suddenly the smell was gone. I had a deep gut feeling that something dramatic was going to happen at any moment. All at once I was wrenched astrally into the air, and for a moment I blacked out from shock. When I came to, I was totally terrified and yet still curious. For there in front of me was a ghoulish monster. A psychic demon.

This monster was beginning to suck all the life force out of my astral body. As I looked over to my physical body it was becoming paler by the moment. I knew that if I did not get back into my physical body, it would be too late and I would then be at the mercy of this psychic vampire! It glowed a darkish red with tints of jet black flickering through it like oily smoke. It was huge and exerted tremendous influence over my mind, which was still in a state of deep shock. I was trying to come to terms with what was happening. Without warning it expanded in size and glowed more intensely. Slowly, it began to take on a human-like figure! Then I realized that this thing wanted *my* body! It wanted my very soul! The monster seemed to 'belong' to that house – was closely connected with it. Could that murder I witnessed from all those years ago have something to do with what was happening to me? Then I knew this foul apparition was linked to the murderer. It was acting out the entire event all over again. Had there been other victims of this gruesome assassin?

For some reason the monster wanted me either out of the house or dead. I realized it was threatened by my psychic awareness. Suddenly I had the sensation of being wrenched hold of again – then the feeling of being squeezed. I felt like an orange put through a juicing machine. Then it hurled me to the floor, but I bounced lightly off and hit the ceiling. I did not feel any physical pain because I was in my astral body. But I did feel an overwhelming sense of tiredness and shock.

The thought returned that if I did not get back into my body, this would be the end of Peter Lee. I would physically die. I could sense all the vital signs in my physical body becoming dangerously low. I would end up discarnate and psychically damaged, an earthbound spirit, doomed to roam the world for centuries. So, mustering all that was left of my feeble strength, I prayed a special prayer to fight back. The attack on me increased and I felt as if I was being pressed into the ground, crushed into nothingness. I could take no more. I screamed a psychic scream. While I was thinking *this is the end, and, bloody hell, what a way to go*, a great light came out of nowhere and filled the room, revitalizing me. It then concentrated itself upon the foul psychic monstrosity, as if to destroy it. But I knew that the light was also making it whole again. In the psychic sense, energy is never destroyed – it only changes form and quality.

With a great flash I was back in my body. Immediately I woke up to find myself in a cold, clammy sweat. Then I heard a distant scream. An unearthly scream. The voice of that monster as it perished! The sense of evil faded away. I fell back into a dreamless sleep.

In the morning I woke to the aroma of freshly made

coffee and a cooked breakfast, and the welcome sparkle of a new spring day. Nature was in full swing and the world outside the window, with the sunlight pouring in, seemed a far cry from the horrors of the night before. As I walked into the kitchen, my friend, without knowing the irony of the question, said, 'Did you sleep well, Peter? No bad dreams, I hope.'

I was about to reply, but something inside told me to hold back. My friend continued, 'You know, I had a funny dream last night, a very strange one – oh, well . . .'

'What did you dream?' I blurted out.

'Oh, it's nothing of any consequence. Just my over-active imagination. After all, a dream is just a dream.'

So I let it drop. I wonder if he had any sense of what happened? Even today I am still wondering about that experience and trying to understand on deeper levels why I, in particular, came face to face with that living nightmare. At least the power of the light and good overcomes the darkness and the chaotic.

Do you ever read detective novels? I used to when I had the time. What I am going to tell you now might turn any detective novelist green for it would make a perfect plot. That it actually happened makes it quite frightening, for it is a look behind the scenes at the intrigue and backstabbing of politics in that constant trouble-spot, the Middle East, where any disturbance could affect the whole security of the Western world.

I received a telephone call asking me to do a reading for a client who would be unable to visit me due to security risks. This was nothing new – I have many clients who prefer to stay within the protection of their own four walls. Some of them are very rich, even kings and princes. Others are poor and fugitives from death in their own countries, while others are anxious to keep their business to themselves. But few people can keep their business from me if they ask me to do a reading. Anyway, I arranged a time to go to see this client.

The next evening the telephone rang. 'You remember, Mr Lee, you and I have an appointment tonight? A car will come for you *now*.' The voice at the other end was abrupt. As I put down the receiver I suspected something fishy was going on, but once again my curiosity got the better of me. Yet I knew I had to stay on my guard at all costs. There are many ways of using one's psychic abilities as a form of self-defence, though I hoped I would not be forced to use them. People's minds, even when aggressors, are sacred. But we all have buttons that, if pushed the right way, leave us as helpless as a baby. The mind is all-powerful.

My front door bell shocked me into action, and I picked up the intercom. A hard, husky voice came through in faltering English. 'We shall wait outside, now, Mr Lee. Please hurry.' I felt like James Bond and Modesty Blaise all rolled into one. As I walked down the stairs to the front door, I made a little web of psychic protection.

When I stepped out into the cold, blustery night, I saw a large black American limousine with tinted glass. It had an ominous gleam underneath the street lights. Two tall, very large Arab gentlemen stood by the back door, immaculately dressed in Savile Row suits. But they had a kind of look on their faces as if they kept long knives down their trousers. From the bulges in their pockets I sensed petite but lethal handguns. Death couched in style.

The driver of this long limousine drove as if he was a demonic coachman with souls destined for hell. One of the 'escorts' was picking his shiny white teeth with a gold toothpick.

Then I found myself outside an impressive building near Queens Gate, which had been expertly renovated. We entered the foyer and there, in the middle of a beautiful black-and-white checked marble floor, stood a most beautiful brass lift. It shone with a deep, satisfying gleam. The interior was mahogany and what looked like kid leather with two large mirrors framed in brass.

The whole building was silent in a strange and disturbing way. I had heard no sound and had seen no other person than my guards, whom I nicknamed Tweedledum and Tweedledee. The lift stopped, and without warning a blindfold was tied securely over my eyes. We began to walk down stairs, up stairs, and then out into the open air, then down more stairs and up again in the lift. I think they were trying to confuse me. I was then escorted into a room, and the blindfold was removed. It was dark. I heard a door slam, then voices, and the lights came on. I was in a waiting room full of cane furniture and many expensively rare house plants. The room was painted a dark tree green. It was very restful.

I knew someone was spying on me through a hole in the wall, so I picked up a magazine and began to read. Suddenly someone came into the room. A very beautiful woman sat down in a chair opposite me. She smiled alluringly – perhaps a distraction? I ignored her politely and when I looked up again she was gone. I was in that room for close to an hour. I was then ushered by a housekeeper down a long plush hallway into another room, much larger and redolent of great wealth and prestige. The room had a high ceiling painted in the Baroque manner. As I looked closer, I could discern that the paintings were in fact panels attached to the ceiling. My clairvoyance told me they were the genuine article. Long dark red velvet curtains fell to the floor, covering huge arched windows. Large Persian carpets hung on the walls; one huge one covered almost the entire floor. My client was something of an expert on art as well as a good investor. The furniture was genuine Regency, all excellent examples. I sat down and studied the large and impressive writing desk that was obviously the nerve-centre of my client's affairs. Presently, a door opened, and the client walked in, flanked by Tweedledum and Tweedledee.

I stood up and he beckoned me to sit down under the Turner. The two Tweedles stood in the corner, staring into space. My client's English was not very good, so we spoke in German. Psychically I told him that he was a doctor of medicine – which was correct – he was in good health and had a considerable hunger for power, and although he had a lot already, he wanted more. I reminded him of the old saying, 'Power corrupts. Absolute power corrupts absolutely.'

He told me that he had long considered that saying, and assumed it must only apply to those who fail in their designs to gain power. He told me that power corrupts even the angels, so he was not really that concerned about it. I said I was sure that he was no angel. At this he smiled – a slow smile that crept around the corners of his mouth as if it was afraid of his face. It was obvious to me that this man was someone extremely powerful in the Middle East. He was not Mohammed, but he could probably move mountains.

I predicted for him that he was going to exercise his power in a particular Middle East country, and that I felt it was going to be Iran, mainly furthering his personal fortunes and ambitions at the cost of the ordinary people. I told him he would be responsible for introducing an ultra right-wing government that would depose through a military coup the then regime which was liberally minded and intent on improving the lot of the common people.

It was as if there was some type of psychic Gordian knot that I was unravelling. I felt the whole security of the Middle East was at risk, as well as that of the world at large. He was eventually going to meddle with world affairs on a large scale. The government he was going to install would be of a highly religious nature, extremely orthodox and very dogmatic. I said that this government, backed up by military might, would create a regime of terror. All the good previously done at great cost of human sacrifice and money would now be ripped away. I told him that the most negative sects of the Islamic religion would gain a greater hold than ever before, harming those believers in Islam who were quiet and gentle at heart.

I said I saw young children dying in the battlefields under the flag of Iran – little-boy soldiers carved up on the fields of death for the designs of an evil figurehead. Iran, I said, would make war on its neighbours, under this hard-line regime. It would be many years, however, before this right-wing regime could be destroyed. I felt that when my client lost interest, the government would collapse and heads would roll. Except for my client, all those directly involved would be brought to justice on national and international levels. They would have the vilification of the entire world heaped upon them, and those who had supported them would turn and spit in their faces. I said to my client that there might be some major world incident sparked off in the coastal waters adjoining Iran and Iraq. This threat would quickly be deflated as war on a horrific scale might have involved the United States of America's intervention, and a mini-nuclear confrontation would be averted. My client suppressed his obvious shock.

Before things got out of hand, peace in the Middle East would be achieved, but it would not last a very long time. Long enough, however, for a stable and liberal government to rule Iran intelligently.

Then a vision came to me. I saw the then leader of Iran running away into the night. I felt he was going to Europe. Where in Europe? It came – he was escaping to France. All that this man had laboured to build for the good of his country was destroyed, smashed to pieces; no one would give him any help. His clothes were covered in blood! Someone he loved was dead.

As I told this to my client, he began to laugh. I thought he was laughing at what I was saying, for to him it might seem ridiculous. In fact, he was laughing with grim pleasure. It was what he wanted to know.

I sensed that my client had a lot of pro-Nazi sympathies, and that he only paid lip-service to Islam as a cover so he could get what he wanted. I said to him that this coup, which historically would be the second in Iran after the Shah, would prove successful in all its aims. But I told him to beware of a religious figurehead, for he could be dangerous to its long-term aims. The reading ended as abruptly as it began. My client had become deadly serious. The room took on a chilly atmosphere. This man, my client, had a very dark and sinister aura.

Next he paid me my fee, but beckoned me to stay seated. After hardly speaking at all during the reading, he now began to talk almost non-stop in a very aggressive and manic way, mentioning Hitler and the Jews a few garbled times. Eventually quietening down, he ordered coffee for us both. He sat back without saying anything until the coffee arrived. I had a feeling that if I wanted to leave, I would be dissuaded by force or even violence, and I began to feel rather angry. The coffee was served in the traditional way by a girl with entrancing eyes.

'Do you recall how you predicted this second coup, Mr Lee?'

'Yes, of course,' I replied carefully.

He smiled. 'Well, I and my many associates comprise that "second coup". Thank you for telling me that we shall be victorious in our goals. It makes me very pleased to know that.' My client continued, 'You have done extremely well tonight, Mr Lee. Yes, extremely well. I was told by a good friend that you are always right. Now I know that to be true.'

I smiled back. Something told me not to touch the coffee.

'I feel so much better, now that we can go ahead.' He said it innocently, as though he was going on a picnic, not on a violent rampage with religious fanatics and clever manipulators determined to rule and reap with an iron fist. I stood up to go. The Tweedles moved towards me. My client barked a command in Farsi. They stopped on the spot.

My client escorted me to the door, but just before I left the room, he pulled me to one side. 'Peter, I have a favour to ask of you. Until all this takes place, we consider you under a vow of complete and utter secrecy . . . I do hope you understand, my friend.' His quiet tone contained a threat. I smiled and told him not to worry about me, turning to leave.

'Oh, Peter,' he said. 'One more thing. You do travel by underground sometimes?'

'Occasionally, if I have to,' I replied.

'Well,' came his reply, 'if you talk about this meeting

to anyone, then you'll most definitely find out what it's like to fall under one of those trains.'

Without hesitation I believed him. Back in the black limousine I was escorted home again by the two Tweedles.

But what of my mysterious client? Perhaps his tall figure with piercing eyes is there somewhere in the background, reaping his rewards from the coup he planned in Queens Gate.

Often I am consulted by representatives of large international businesses. One of the most interesting consultations concerned the abuse of a large loan that was lent to a major world power through the auspices of an international money consortium. The country concerned is geographically very close to the United Kingdom. The consortium, desperate for reliable information, had failed to find anything through its own devices, and so came to me. Without some kind of help they were worried that the situation could turn into a nasty international incident, with the newspapers going to town. Heads could roll in Great Britain, Europe and the United States of America! This consortium had come to me before, so they had trust in me. Their problem was indeed serious. They really wanted to know the truth and how they could reclaim that part of the loan they were owed as payment for handling the deal. Their percentage was a very large sum of money. Respected members of the country's highly controversial, supposedly socialist, government had abused this money for their own ends. The consortium also wanted to know what they could do to help protect the bank that orchestrated the loan and issued the money. They also wanted to know who had the money now.

This consortium is a very powerful force in its own right; perhaps private justice would be meted out in some dark corner to the culprits. While I was helping this consortium I was followed and threatened with death by that country's secret service. They told me to keep out of the whole affair, but I did not. I was employed to work on a serious problem. Through the use of my clairvoyance, the truth of the matter became very clear to my client.

This country still has its socialist president, but its recent elections smashed a great hole in the socialist wall of strength. To be used as testament to the demonstration of truth through prediction is indeed humbling. Predictions, besides being useful for people, are a dramatic way of proving the reality of the psychic world.

A murder always grabs the interest of the public, and more so when a child is involved. There seems to be a grim fascination with the act of one human being exterminating another. Tragic and often inexplicable murder is the strangest aspect of man's inhumanity to man. It is complex, often without motive, reason or rhyme.

But what would you do if justice is diverted, even though you have discovered the truth? Well, if you are psychic, legally you cannot do a thing. A psychic's testimony is often ignored as evidence. You can only be thankful that your psychic gifts were good enough to reveal to you, at least, the real truth of the case.

This actually happened to me, and it seemed as though justice was not taken to its full conclusion. This was when I became involved in the chilling Mark Tildsley murder case. Mark lived in the Wokingham area and was a very popular little boy. Polite, helpful –

it was difficult to imagine anyone wanting to kill him. But, tragically, that was the case. In June 1984, after I had received frantic calls from Mark's mother on my answering machine, I contacted her.

Mrs Tildsley asked if I would help uncover the facts about her missing son, and, of course, the identity of the murderer. For she was convinced that Mark was dead; and a mother's intuition is seldom wrong. When I first spoke to her on the telephone, I sensed that Mark was definitely dead, but the rest was shrouded in mystery. Because so much was unknown and unresolved, I consented to help the Tildsley family unravel the mystery around Mark's death. Later on, the local newspaper asked if they could cover my investigation. They did this extremely well and honestly, without any undue sensationalism. They were quite sensitive to the needs of the Tildsley family. The case soon attracted the attention of the national newspapers.

I drove down from London to see Mr and Mrs Tildsley, and clairvoyantly I described the person that I knew to be responsible for this ghastly act. My description was in fact very different to the one first given by the press and on television. The one I gave was of a very slim youth who would have been a local and certainly would know of the Tildsley family. To this day, I am absolutely certain of it. Unfortunately, because of the very private circumstances surrounding the murder, I cannot come out and identify the murderer. According to the police, Mark is still classified as missing. That is not the case! When I spoke to the Tildsleys, they seemed to be taking everything extremely well. In reality they had repressed the shock so much that at that time it had not consciously hit them. The true grief was yet to come. Bitter tears were shed behind closed doors . . .

I felt that I should go to where Mark had last been

seen and then divine the events that took place. I drove around, letting my psychic energies take me where they would. I came to a large field where I sensed a funfair had been held. I opened the long wooden gate, closing it carefully behind me. As I walked into the field it was a lot larger than I expected, and was quite beautiful. Little wild flowers dotted the verdant green. The wind rustled high in the branches of old and wise oak trees that grew straight and strong. I took in the atmosphere of the place, tuning in to the patterns of nature that flowed through it. I sensed birds nesting in the hedgerow and butterflies drinking the early evening dew. As the shadows from the clouds grew and the first calm of evening touched the field, I knew that it was time to start.

I began psychically to see the funfair form in the atmosphere. The noise of happy children, stalls that sold trinkets. A shooting gallery, the smell of candy-floss and toffee-apples. The mechanical tune of the merry-go-round. I knew that Mark's vibrations were amongst this memory. I began to move around, involving myself in what I saw as if I was at the fair too. I began to call out to Mark's vibrations with my mind, so to speak, and slowly I began to pick them up, weak at first, but then they grew stronger. Mark's spirit wanted his murderer to be exposed.

The clicking of the local reporter's camera did not bother me, although at one point he kept asking me questions and I had to tell him not to disturb me. Mark's vibrations were becoming more precise all the time. From out of the garble of psychic images I began to see him within the psychic imprint left by the funfair. His image then disappeared. I saw him again, over in the far corner of the field with a taller and much older boy. Then suddenly they were gone and the image of the funfair vanished into the psychic memory bank. I reached into my coat pocket and pulled out a pendulum, in order to dowse the area for the direction in which Mark went. Slowly the pendulum took me in the direction of the two figures. Slowly, step by step, the vibrations increased, with the pendulum swinging in mad, crazy circles until for some inexplicable reason it shattered into many pieces. Had it picked up catastrophe?

Psychically I heard Mark's voice. The words were indistinct, but there was an unmistakable sense of urgency. What was going on? Was Mark in a state of terror at that point? I had to find out. Death was in the air. I followed my clairvoyance and came upon a hole, not very big, but a hole in the hedgerow where the two boys, Mark and his murderer, had gone. I was absolutely sure the person I saw psychically with Mark was the killer. To my surprise I found that I could fit easily enough through the hole in the hedgerow. This started a whole lot of questions racing through my mind.

I shouted to the reporter to bring the car round and meet me on the road. Presently we were off again, searching this flat and damp countryside for the truth, for the answer to the macabre riddle: where was Mark's body?

We drove on for a while, until we passed a long narrow lane. 'Stop the car here. Now drive down there, quick!' We drove down the lane. It was rocky and covered with undergrowth. We came to a small bridge, a railway line, and then to a clearing. More trees and then another clearing. I stopped there. Vibrations came flooding off a hillside directly in front of me. Vibrations of a murderous struggle. A final blow that ended young Mark's life. I could smell the trickle of warm blood. But something told me to return to the bridge and walk back step by step. I asked the reporter to wait where he was until I returned. I walked back to the bridge and started to use my psychometry on it. I first picked up the approach of two people, one tall, one small, both young. I sensed the small person was worrying or crying. The two people had been arguing. It had to be Mark with the murderer.

I then followed the psychic images that I was picking up. They were like a three-dimensional television picture. I began to see at last the events unfolding as they actually happened. An instant replay, so to speak. As I crossed the bridge I saw the older boy push Mark. Mark hit back. The older boy laughed. As I approached the railway line, there was more arguing and blows were exchanged. It seemed that, regardless of his size, Mark could give as good as he got. One of his punches had hurt the older boy, but not seriously. As I came into the first clearing, a full-scale fist fight had developed. Both boys were bruised and slightly bleeding. Mark ran away through the trees, into the second clearing and up on to the hillside. The tall boy ran after Mark. A struggle of some sort broke out on the hill. A struggle that proved to be fatal. An idiotic and tragic waste of a young life.

I also felt that Mark could be buried somewhere on or near the hillside. The vibrations of violent death literally screamed off it. The psychic din was deafening. Unfortunately, even with my help, Mark's body was never found. Whether it was by chance or not, I wonder if anyone will ever really know.

Later on I was approached by the Thames Valley Police. They asked me if I would be able to build an Identikit, based on my clairvoyant description of the young murderer at large. Everyone in the neighbourhood wanted to shield the Tildsley family from further harm. This was perfectly natural in such a close-knit community where everyone cared about everyone else. Even the local police were friendly, relaxed and extremely diligent. They did not have the cold mentality of a vast metropolitan police-force. But I feel, without any doubt at all, that Mark's murderer still lives in the area.

It is unfortunate that this particular case will never come to the light of society's justice; but it has already been brought to the light of God's. No one ever escapes the justice of natural law.

Chapter 8
Readings and Results

I would like to share with you a few readings that are good examples of the type I get from both first-time clients and those who have come to me on a regular basis, year in, year out. The readings usually last between forty and sixty minutes, and I work from holding an object belonging to the client. So now let us enter the private worlds of some of my clients, their hopes, dreams, fears and desires.

A short time ago a very strong and determined lady came to look for help concerning her future, especially a business venture and the health of her mother.

'You have been away somewhere, not just on a holiday, but somewhere that has, for a time, been quite permanent. Is this right?'

'Yes,' the lady replied.

'In your life, while you have lived abroad, there has been a big break or separation that has hurt you emotionally. Is that right?'

'Yes, very much.' She looked at me with sadness as she spoke the words.

'I feel that there has been a great division of property, and all the haggling over material things has drained you of a lot of energy. This relationship that broke had dragged on and on. It was as though this man was becoming a ball and chain. Is that right?'

She nodded in agreement, and sighed.

'I feel that you put a lot of energy into this relationship, but it did not have any solid effect. You were doing an awful lot of waiting around for this chap. You were in the Middle East when this relationship fell to pieces, and it seems that after a while the environment became too much for you. A link with the United States comes in now, and for some reason it is connected with this ex-boyfriend of yours. Your ex-boyfriend is American. This relationship is not over with in any way. In fact it is just in the early stages. A lot more must pass between you both. You haven't seen the last of him. I feel that you don't know where he is or how to contact him, but he can contact you without any real trouble. He is a man with many resources at his fingertips.'

The lady smiled at me. 'Everything you said so far is correct. I'm a little nervous about the relationship starting off again, though.'

'Don't worry about that. It will look after itself,' I said, trying to reassure her. 'I see a situation in which you were organizing for others. When you were handling other people's affairs. Does this make sense?'

'Yes, it certainly does,' she said.

'It has a lot to do with business dealings and people who travel abroad a great deal. Some of them are very important people. People of great substance. You've also handled these people's affairs in the United Kingdom. I now see a house, a beautiful house, in rolling countryside. There is a great sense of peace and tranquillity around it. It is in the English countryside. The house is very big, spacious, and I feel it belongs to the man that you will end up marrying in the not too distant future. There has been a major redevelopment in all your business arrangements recently. This will

139

indicate a major change in direction and a new start in your life. There has been a waiting period around this, as if you are hoping for something particular to happen. Things are taking off slowly. There is, though, a middleman involved in this venture. This middleman is going to speed things up very quickly, and you are also owed a large amount of money because of it. This money will be returned to you, plus extra that you didn't expect! You are very much a loner, and at the moment you enjoy being alone. It is as though you need this. You feel secure on your own, you are having trouble in opening up your emotions. This is a time when you are getting things together. You have lost a considerable amount of money in the past, and I can tell you now that through some other means, I'm not sure what, that loss is going to be made up to you. It is as though you only want to move one step at a time. You are not at rock bottom, but if you do anything rash, you will hit rock bottom. But if you continue on this path, things are going to improve greatly.

'For quite some time you are going to avoid all deep emotional involvements. England makes you very unhappy, but you are unsure where to go. People from the past are going to invite you to work overseas. Eventually you will go to live in a very sunny climate. You will feel at home in this place, as though you always belonged there. Friends will surround you. A business venture developed abroad by you will make you secure for life, comfortable, but not very rich. In a few years, the man whom you can love totally will come into your life. He will be a man who loves the countryside, but lives in the city. Eventually you and he will live in the country. It's only a matter of months before you leave England. Soon there will be a definite lack of connection between England and yourself.

'You will meet this man, who was previously married. He is the man for you. Your life will totally change. You will feel consolidated, and you will have immediate and complete harmony with this man for the rest of your natural life. You will spend the last years of your life on a coast, where you will start to write, and your life will be worthwhile to the media. You will publish your life story.

'Did you have a difficult or complicated father? He is still alive, but I feel he is away. He divorced your mother and married someone else and I feel he wishes you were a boy? Is that right?' My client smiled and agreed. 'I feel that your father is insecure about his will and testament. There will be complications over it; you will receive a large part of the inheritance, but someone will contest the will, and they will lose their case in court. I feel that your mother is quite ill, and I can tell you that she will die within the year, or at least the next eighteen months. Your mother married someone else. You may have to be a pillar of strength to this man, even if you don't know him that well. Don't worry about your problems so much, otherwise you may collapse from mental exhaustion.'

The reading ended with the lady feeling very much better, and far more confident about her future. During the reading, Trotsky had sat on her lap and refused to budge, and at the end of the reading she brought out of her bag a little gift for him – some strips of smoked salmon. That cat has all the luck!

Now I would like to move on to a reading I did for a most unhappy man. He was truly tragic, for he was making his life hell by his own attitudes. He was in a deep state of negativity, and I felt that though he had come to me for help, he wouldn't act upon what I said.

'You came to this country, and then for some mysterious reason you left again in a hurry, and then returned here when you felt more secure. Is that right?'

'Yes, that is right,' said the man, somewhat shocked.

'I feel that seven years ago you and your wife divorced each other. Is that right?'

The man was even more shocked. 'Yes,' he said. He stuttered slightly.

'Your wife then left England, and you haven't seen her since. That causes you a lot of pain. You are still in love with her . . . you should try to overcome this feeling . . . another woman will come into your life. Your marriage was a very violent one. Your wife missed her freedom and friends, and I feel that once she divorced you, she went to live in North America . . . I feel Canada, yes, she went to live in Canada. You even went so far as trying to follow her and convince her that things could work out. You must really try to forget this woman. The memories that you have of her will only screw you up and ruin the rest of your life.

'I feel that your health is getting worse and you are doing nothing about it. You are very unlucky in relationships with women. There have been a large number of short relationships. You have been let down by all your friends. I feel that you are far too easygoing, and are very unsure of making changes in your life. You drink far too much; you drink at home, alone. If you are not careful you will become addicted to drink – it will kill you. You do not assert yourself, and give too much of yourself to other people. A married couple seem to be your best and most real friends. They are connected with your work. You should trust them more. They will help you a great deal. But at the moment there is no one to listen to your troubles. I feel that you want to meet women, but you don't give yourself the chance.

'You have a cousin who has great worries about her child. She needs your help immediately. The child is quite ill, and her husband is not faithful. You are going to settle down again. You did have the chance to marry again, but it fell through. A new chance is coming your way. Within the next two and a half years, you will meet the lady that you will marry. But a word of warning: before this, you will meet a young, good-looking girl who will use you and treat you like a slave. With a false face, she will be all smiles, but she will be interested only in what she can get. The lady who will be your wife will be between thirty-two and forty-eight, and will have been divorced for at least nine years. She will have children and run a large and busy house, and in this environment you will begin to feel at last comfortable and at peace with yourself. This relationship will move slowly at first, and it will be continuous, no breaks in any way. Love will have finally come to stay.

'You used to know how to enjoy yourself – learn again. If you give too much of yourself to other people, you will destroy your life, your personality and your reputation. You find it very hard to save your money, and if you lend to anyone over the next year, you will lose an awful lot of money. I will make a final warning about this young woman: don't have anything to do with her. Everything I say to you is going to happen, but you can improve your lot in life by getting out and about. You must learn to know the difference between the genuine people and the sharks. Until your wife-to-be comes along, please be careful about how you conduct your life. Cut down on the booze. You should have more faith in higher things.'

After I had finished the reading, the man sat in silence, staring into space. Slowly he began to cry. I let him cry. All the loneliness and tension, the heartache and sorrow, came out of him. Twenty minutes later he left, with a new direction in life, knowing that he could change his life for the better, but sadly I felt that he would do nothing about it.

The next reading concerns a lady who is trapped between a stale marriage and the desire for a lasting loving relationship. She has trouble with her family, and yet desires above all to have freedom for herself.

'I sense a great gap between you and your husband, both in the fact that he travels a great deal and you hardly see him, and that there is little love between you. It is as though the love was strangled, and is dying a slow death. The two of you live in the same house, but there is nothing more than that. There have been two major upheavals in your life. You have lived in other countries – in the Middle East and in France. Is that correct?'

The lady said that all of it was correct so far, so I continued. 'Your marriage is going to fall apart quite soon. I feel that you will end the marriage. Even from the time you were first married there wasn't a lot in common. You married very young; were you eighteen years old when you got married?'

'Yes, Mr Lee. How did you know?' I smiled and said that the psychic knows all.

'In the Middle East did you leave because of a war? I feel that you lived in the Lebanon. This caused a great deal of grief. Did you lose a child at birth?'

The lady sighed. 'Yes, I still think about that baby. She was my first.'

'You have two sons. The older one is OK, but the younger one is under a great deal of pressure. People expect too much of him. His father does not understand him in any way at all. I feel that he will be happiest if he is allowed to follow an artistic vocation. He is very restless, unhappy, and he is slowly coming to terms with the world and himself. He will change schools this year, and he will be happier.

'When he is twenty he will be studying in order to learn his art. He won't become very settled until he is thirty and then after that he will be successful. The older brother is going to travel a great deal for most of his life, and will marry quite soon. There is a great unhappiness in you. You find your husband boring; he is preoccupied with his own life. He is not faithful to you, but he is against divorce, mainly because of tradition. He is quite a selfish man, but he is basically a good man. He wants his family to live life the way he wants them to. I feel that you are having an affair with another man, who is also married. It will stop and start. He cares for you, but he won't leave his wife, even though he says he will. Your real love is still on its way. You could work at your marriage, by making your husband include you in his life.'

The lady interrupted. 'I don't want to save my marriage, Mr Lee. He really is a bastard.'

'You will meet your real love in two years. You will eventually return to France and live there. This will make you very happy within yourself. I feel that your husband doesn't realize how you feel. The man that you will marry will be a tonic, and make you laugh a great deal. He will help you to become passionate again. You will go on a few secret romantic trips with the married man. Yet through friends who live overseas you will meet your future husband.

'Your husband is going to have a serious stomach problem. You should see that he has proper treatment before things are too late. Your sons will be shocked at first when you are divorced, but then they will stand by you. Your present husband will spend his later life alone. You will outlive both of your husbands. As far as your boyfriend is concerned, I do feel that he will see you when he feels like it. For heaven's sake do put some restraint into the affair, otherwise it will cause more heartache than it's worth. Your younger son will need a great deal of encouragement. I feel that there may be violence between him and his father. But that can be averted, if there is a better relationship between the two of them. I feel that in a way, now that the boys are older, your husband wants to forget them.'

As I finished, the lady sighed a great sigh of relief. She was happy with the reading, and felt a lot of what I had said showed her how to conduct her future. She left completely satisfied.

I will always remember one client whose tragic life affected me to the core. She was a young girl, very much in love with a man almost nine years her senior. She wanted to know if she would end up marrying him. I told her that he was not the man for her, and if she persisted in seeing him, she would only end up used, abused and seriously hurt. She became very angry when I told her this, but I reminded her that the truth often hurts and you can't hide behind dreams if they are not based on a reality or wish that can be attained. She left in a storm.

A year later she rang me. She was four months pregnant and she wanted to come for a reading. So she did.

Once again, nothing but warnings and bad news came to me for her. My predictions were not happy ones.

'I have to tell you, that only bad things await you concerning this child and the man. You are fortunate that you have youth on your side and that basically you have a strong personality. So I want you to brace yourself for what I am about to predict for you . . . firstly, the child that you are now carrying will die in a cot death.' She began to cry. 'I'm sorry to say such harsh things, but you must hear the truth. Providence may seem cruel, but it is saving you from a far worse fate. I feel that this man wants to take you to Paris to live. If you do, he may eventually try to make you become a prostitute in order to support him. If you continue in a relationship with this man, there is a good chance that he may end up trying to kill you. You can change things if you want to. I can help you overcome this problem, and together we can speak to your parents. I feel that you haven't given your parents a chance, and you should not exclude them from your life any more.'

Understandably she went away upset. I was hoping to hear from her. I didn't for a long time. Then one night there was a soft, pathetic knocking at my front door. It was about a quarter past midnight and the rain was pelting down, and there in the pouring rain she stood timid and frightened. As soon as she saw me, she broke into a cascade of bitter tears. After she had had a hot bath and a couple of brandies, she began to tell me her story.

'Mr Lee, I should have listened to you all along. We went to Paris just like you said we would. Everything went wrong. My baby, well, my baby died six weeks later in a cot death!' She broke down, crying; grief was racking her soul. After she had calmed down a little, she continued, 'He was very nice to me for a while, but he wanted drugs for himself, and he used to beat me up. He made me go on the game. I tried to run away as best I could, but he caught me every time. I became petrified. Then an old lady who lived in a flat across the hall spoke to me one day. She seemed to know what was going on, and said that if I needed any help all I had to do was ask her.'

'Did you take up the lady's offer?' I asked.

'Well, not at first, because I thought that if she got involved he might hurt her. But one night he really beat me up. I got out of the flat. I thought he was going to kill me! I knocked on the old lady's door. She opened it and then dragged me in, locking her door behind her. Then she telephoned someone. About ten minutes later, there was a knock at her door. I thought it was him! She opened the door, and three huge men walked in. She told me these were her sons. She spoke to them about what had happened, and what I had told her. They left. I found out that all three of them were policemen.'

She went on to tell me that this lady's sons arrested the man who had treated her so cruelly. The old lady and her family showed her a great deal of kindness. They gave her the money to come back to England. She was going back to her parents but she didn't have the courage. Thus she came to me.

Everything turned out well in the end. Her parents stood by her, she finished off her education and met a young man. They are now engaged. I predicted that for her as well. She comes to see me with her fiancé, and I know that her life from now on will be very happy and secure.

A friend of mine has a house in Cornwall. When he

and his wife first moved in, everything seemed all right. Then after about a month, strange and frightening things began to take place. The house was haunted, by not one but four ghosts! Tables began to move, cups were found smashed on the floor, heavy footsteps and talking could be heard on the stairs during day or night. The situation became so bad it almost destroyed my friend's marriage. Then the unfortunate couple came to see me. I am usually very sceptical about hauntings and poltergeists. More ghosts haunt people's minds than they do houses. They told me everything that had gone on – how my friend's wife was standing at the front door when something knocked her on to the ground and began to drag her out of the house. After dwelling on this, I became convinced of the psychic reality of the hauntings and went down to the strange house in Cornwall. It was a small three-bedroomed cottage about two hundred years old. A great confusion of vibrations streamed off the building. Something truly evil had taken place there. Murder, and, to my utter amazement, ritual black magic! People two hundred years ago with confused and warped minds had sacrificed a young couple in a horrific and insane ritual murder!

As I entered the cottage, I felt a swarm of psychic malevolence. The evil energy in the place was threatened by me. I decided to perform an exorcism. I told my friends that if they wanted to keep the house, then they should do as I asked. First, I began to protect my friends and myself with psychic energy through prayer, then with my clairvoyance I reached out to make contact. The house was full of four pathetic earthbound spirits, the young murdered couple and two older men. I was surprised how easy it was for me to convince the spirits of the young couple that they were earthbound, and that they were free. I told them to leave the cottage and find eternal rest, and they went!

The other two were not so easy. These ghosts were raging, angry and violent. It took me sixteen hours of constant prayer until, through my clairvoyance once again, they became restrained. They refused to leave; they did not like the way my friends had 'messed' things up in the house. At that point cups, plates, chairs and even a table were hurled at me, so I summoned all my energy together and asked that they be cast out of the house for ever and that divine justice, natural law, would take its effect.

I felt that we should leave the house and return in the morning. This we did. The next morning was bright and sunny, and the flowers in the garden of the cottage seemed to have more life in them. The house had been cleansed and purified. The ghosts had gone. As we went out into the back garden, I felt drawn to a small area of bushes. There was a grave . . . I suddenly felt further trouble. I was worn out. I told my friends that they should get the local priest to consecrate the grave. They did that. Now, I am happy to say, the house is normal in every way.

On another occasion I found myself acting as the godfather to a little boy. After the family and friends had returned to the apartment, which overlooks Hyde Park, for the christening tea, I was asked by the mother of the child if I could use my powers to find her mother's handbag. She was rather nervous about asking me to do such a thing outside working hours. But there really is no such thing for a psychic, and anyway, the handbag contained some tablets that her mother had to take for her heart. I said, off the cuff, that it was in the master bedroom, under the bed. One of the children present had hidden it there for a prank. As soon as the bag was found, everyone at the reception knew about it, and I was then inundated with appointments for readings from 'the Hyde Park set'.

Every now and then I am asked by a client to trace someone. One situation that springs to mind was when a young man came to me to know if he could discover who his real parents were. As a baby he was put into an orphanage, and from the age of five he had gone from foster home to foster home, until he finally settled down with a family that he could relate to. This family had been very good to him. They had given him love and security, financed him through university to do a law degree, but still something was missing. At first I was in a quandary as to the correctness of the son meeting his natural parents after all these years. Finally I decided that it would do no harm. It might be painful for a while for a lot of people, but in the end the young man would benefit.

'I feel that your parents were in a situation where they could not keep you. Your mother gave birth to you when she was seventeen. Both she and your father came from extremely well-to-do families, and your parents were literally stopped from seeing each other. After you were born your mother was sent away to Switzerland to a clinic. Your parents were very much in love with each other. Your father, still a young man then, hunted your mother down. It took him a year to find her. They escaped and went to live in northern Australia. Once there, they were able to set up home together. It was there that they were married. Two years later both of them were dead. They had friends there, but the friends

151

didn't know much about their past. They died in a car accident. Their car skidded on a bridge and went over the edge into a ravine or gully. Their graves are in a graveyard just outside the little town where they lived.

'That is all I can tell you. I hope you are not too upset, but I can only tell you what I discover and what comes to me.'

The young man looked at me. At first he did not know what to do. But then he said that he felt more at peace and he would visit their graves, so I gave him, as best I could, the name of the town. He did visit the graves, and he wrote to me, saying that he was thinking of settling down in Australia, for in the great expanse of that wild country he felt right at home. Toby was the young man's name, and I believe that he married a pretty young girl whose family lived only a few miles from where his parents once had their home.

Some time ago I did a psychic exhibition at the Cunard Hotel. I do not often do exhibitions, because you can find yourself involved with a lot of cranks and weird people. I have no desire to be associated with the lunatics of the psychic world! But in this particular situation I did relent, because a person of great integrity was involved. Among the numerous people at the short demonstration sittings was a young woman, and the first thing that came to me was that she was married to a very interesting man, a big-time manager and agent of some top names in the international showbusiness scene. He appeared, though, to be a rather happy-go-lucky guy who, regardless of his success, had a very carefree attitude to the world.

During the course of the reading I kept picking up a very negative older lady who was attached to the husband. This older lady was the young woman's mother-in-law. As the reading went on, the stifling sensation of deep depression and suicide flooded over me. It was so draining! The older woman was giving in to every little problem that life brought her way, and was bringing herself down terribly. I related all of this to my client, and she said that it was indeed her mother-in-law.

She looked at me and said, 'I try to avoid her like grim death, Mr Lee, but of course I can't. I see her all the time, and she makes me depressed.' I gave her a few words of encouragement and then she continued, 'When I go with my husband to see her, I get very upset. Her house is full of negative feelings. I'm sure she is suicidal.'

Through this lady, I kept picking up a very famous psychic, and it turned out that her suicidal mother-in-law managed this psychic's business affairs. All through the readings that I did for this lady, the mother-in-law's desire for suicide grew in intensity. I tried to urge my client, on many occasions, to do what she could to stop the older lady from taking her own life. I even suggested that my client should spend a Christmas with her disturbed mother-in-law, although she was very much against it. But, in fact, they did spend Christmas together, which helped to prolong the older woman's life. My client told me recently that her mother-in-law had written to her saying that she intended committing suicide . . .

Unless something is done quickly, there is no doubt in my mind – the mother-in-law is a very determined woman and she will kill herself in a tragic but dramatic way.

*

153

Some years ago, a very vibrant young man came to see me, with a friend, for a reading. At that time I was doing readings in Crouch End, in North London. Like all young men, he was of course more interested in his future, but first I went through his past and present. What a future my prediction foretold! I mentioned to him that he was connected with politics, which he said was right. He was absolutely amazed, for about a year before he had become a member of a major political party. I said to him that in a very short time he would be serving in public office. He was taken aback at first. He was once again amazed, for he had just put himself forward to contest a place on the local council.

Then I said that eventually he would go on to play a very prominent part in the government of this country, Great Britain. He served as a local councillor for several years and then became a Member of Parliament. He is now a very influential and prominent member of the SDP-Liberal Alliance. Psychically, I believe that he will come into greater power as a member of the actual government, sooner than many people realize.

Chapter 9
America! The Sunny Side Up!

America has always held a deep and abiding fascination for me, with its myriad and mixed cultures all blending in different ways to unite in one identity. In the last few years I have been flying back and forth between London and the United States, mainly at my clients' requests. I usually go for six weeks a year. My clients are basically situated in the New Jersey area close to the University of Princeton.

I have also stayed in the United States for periods of a few months at a time, specially when I wanted a change of scenery. I had a small but regular group of clients, and I was successful enough not to become broke. My practice in the United States of America began quite by accident, but looking back at it now, I can see that it was the work of higher forces and my spirit guides. I had some associates from Manhattan who were connected with the film industry in a big way. It was in New York City that my practice really grew.

My New York practice is now very busy, but my Princeton-New Jersey practice is more relaxed and easygoing. I soon discovered that my reputation spread further afield, and on one occasion I found myself in Atlanta, Georgia. There I was in the Deep South of the USA to appear on a radio chat show, where people phoned in, and I would talk to them about psychic things, as well as giving predictions for them over the air.

I had one very wealthy client who flew me into Atlanta by private jet. After I finished the chat show, I was coming out of the studio with the very charming lady who had interviewed me. I said, 'I bet the Ku-Klux-Klan are outside waiting for me!' I meant this to be a joke as they don't care for psychics, but this lady, God bless her, became very worried, and said, 'Oh, holy smoke! You don't think so, do you? I'd better get security!' But before I could explain, an armed contingent of security guards escorted me from the building, on to the quiet streets. There was a rather motley welcoming committee – two stray dogs. No burning crosses. No white hooded men. Just one empty street, with a slight wind blowing the trash. I felt rather let down.

I had a very interesting suggestion made to me by one client who is also an excellent journalist on the staff of the London *Standard*, Ms Rosalind Russell. Rosalind is the deputy editor of the 'Ad Lib' section of the newspaper, which keeps tabs on all that is going on in the London arts, music and entertainment scene.

She suggested that, in association with the then brand-new Virgin Atlantic Airways, owned by millionaire Richard Branson, I should use my reputation and abilities in advertising the airline. I did readings for people on the plane whenever I went to the States. It was highly successful, and I received many free trips to the United States and back, courtesy of the airline. I was treated very well and given VIP service all the time. When I got to Newark Airport, instead of waiting for hours to be seen by Customs, as in the past, I was whisked through the whole procedure in under three minutes.

I received quite a lot of news coverage concerning my aerial predictions, and the whole affair was dubbed 'Fortunes in the Sky'. But I became rather tired of travelling like that, and now I fly to the States only at clients' expense. 1984 and 1985 were very busy years for me in the United States. Many of my clients were seeing me twice or three times a year. Most of those in Princeton are millionaires.

Many are, of course, highly influential, but because of business ethics I cannot talk about them. Some of them are indeed highly exciting and interesting people. The Johnson family, of Johnson & Johnson the famous pharmaceutical company, have a beautiful family mansion in the area.

Princeton is a place that I just fell in love with. I was consulted there by many professors and administrators from the university, as well as well-known artists – especially singers from the prestigious New York Metropolitan Opera.

There is there a strong psychic energy left over from its past. Often I would go for an evening stroll, as is my pleasure after a busy day seeing clients. On one occasion I was walking along a small avenue when I suddenly found myself at the turn of the twentieth century. I observed the people and the fashions of that period with fascination. Princeton had divulged its psychic secrets to me.

Some of the buildings go back at least three hundred years, and the vibrations that stream off them are of immense interest. Some tell of dark secrets, of murders and mayhem, of earthbound spirits and ghosts. Others are just joyful, simple psychic impressions of families living normally in the now distant past.

On the campus of the university there is a most beautiful church. The outside is simple enough, but it is graceful, and one can really sense an energy of worship that is sincere and long-lasting. Many were the hours I spent there in quiet contemplation. I found it was at least one place other than my apartment where I could have the time alone to reflect upon my soul. Often, when the church was empty, some unknown organist would practise there. Quietly I would sneak in and sit in the back row, carried away on the tidal swells and plunging music of Bach. I found this peaceful time of meditation an added boost towards freeing my spirit from any troubles I had, and afterwards I would walk out into the world more alive and sensitive than when I walked in. I would then go to a coffee house and sit with the memory of the music and the aroma of fresh coffee swirling through my senses.

The church went back at least two hundred years, and in times of solitude I often discovered aspects of its past. On one occasion as I was sitting there peacefully I sensed someone sitting next to me. As I looked out of the corner of my eye, I saw a dapper gentleman sitting there quietly. Quickly I realized that he was a person from the spirit world. 'I enjoy this church thoroughly, you know. My daughter was married here. I come back every now and then.' Before I had a chance to ask his name, some loud tourists walked in, and he was gone. I often think that in the stillness of the night that ghostly gentleman returns to enjoy his church, in the peace and quiet, and relive his memories.

As I was getting to know Princeton better, I used to take buses all over the town. In one instance, I was sitting watching the world go by when I noticed a young girl in the seat in front of me in a terrible state of distress. I sensed by my clairvoyance that she felt life was just too much for her to handle. I began to feel the prompting from the spirit world to help her so, carefully,

I approached her. After talking to her for a short time, I made her realize the senselessness of taking her own life. She was only sixteen and had so many good things to look forward to. Then and there I did a prediction for her, touching upon how she was overcome with sadness and misery since her father died and, not being very close to her mother, was at a complete and utter loss.

I told her that I was a professional clairvoyant, and she began to listen seriously, and soon was smiling. Before she got off the bus, I told her that one day she would become a famous singer, and I expect that soon her name will be high in the international pop charts.

Now let us go from Princeton to the hustle, the bustle of the Big Apple – for it seems everyone in the world wants a large bite out of New York!

Often it feels as though it is the heartbeat of America – a fascinating city. Yet it also has all the attributes of many small towns compressed into a larger entity. I always find myself comparing New York to London, maybe because I am London born and bred. London has a certain type of friendliness that New York, at first, does not seem to show. Of course both cities are large, fast-moving places, but London, especially in a psychic sense, does not seem as sinister as New York. In New York one can sense the intrigue lurking behind the corners.

New York has an invisible heartbeat that is sometimes oppressive. It is so obvious that there were times when I felt that I could pull it from the air, or cut it with a knife. It was a definite ectoplasm created in the atmosphere by the constant outpouring of chaos and frenzy that is so common there.

When I first arrived in New York, it was stinking hot. Everyone was reaching for deodorants, long cool drinks, air-conditioning units and portable fans. The city was in a heatwave, like the largest sauna in the world. It remained like this night and day. New York is a city of extremes.

I have an apartment on West 72 Street where I always stay. My apartment building is called Embassy Towers and it has a character all of its own, with an unmistakable sense of flair and service. I struck up an association with the doorman, Rocky. Rocky knew the city inside out, and when I was going out or coming in, and he was not too busy, he would chat to me about the real city. All the characters he knew. How the place had changed. He was in some respects eccentric, and used to stand outside the doors wearing a ten-gallon sheriff's hat, and on his shirt he wore a sheriff's badge! He carried a stick about three feet long that he would bounce from hand to hand, and hidden discreetly he had a revolver. This was Rocky's style. The management adored him. He attracted people to the building just by his personality.

The apartment building is full of famous singers and actors. Many well-known names live above and below me. There are a few well-known writers at the top of the building, and a famous painter has an apartment in the basement.

As people began to hear of me, so did the other tenants. Soon I had several clients living in the same building, and usually great parties burst into life spontaneously after consultations.

The most marvellous, awe-inspiring sight I ever saw in New York – still my favourite, a blend of nature and man's technology – is Manhattan at night from Roosevelt Island. It is just so beautiful that it makes you wonder if you are really in some dark deep canyon at sunset watching the shadows and light playing over the tall rocks and craggy pinnacles.

But the reason I have such special memories of that view is because of the first time I arrived in New York with Virgin. After landing in the United States on the inaugural flight of Virgin Atlantic Airways, making my way through the VIP area I received a call.

I was at that time going to stay with some friends on Long Island, who worked in the movies. I was told on the telephone to forget Long Island for the time being, and come directly to Roosevelt Island because a film was being made there, and the star wanted to see me. He had been trying to catch me in England, but I was always booked up.

So off I went in a clapped-out New York taxi to meet this star and do a reading. The trip through New York's streets was stimulating. I passed a streetside stripper, a man with a dancing monkey, and a riot between two Christians and some Hare Krishnas. The taxi driver talked non-stop all the way. Eventually, after getting lost three times, we got there safely.

There on the island I found an enormous film set. It was a mini-town in its own right. I spent hours waiting to see this man. My friends stressed that it was highly important, and I was told by a messenger from the star that I should not worry because he was paying me a considerable sum by the hour. I began to sense a serious problem, which in the end, thanks to the higher forces, I was able to help this man solve.

I was still suffering from jet-lag, and the man I was going to see was totally drunk in his dressing room (an oversize caravan), and not aware that half the New York

161

film industry was out in the heat waiting for him to make an appearance! He had just been made to reshoot a speech about thirty times, and every time the crew went for a take something seemed to go wrong . . . the agony of film-making.

The director had given up, and all the other actors and the technical crew were in what could be mildly called a state of agitation. Only the caterers seemed to be in control; they were the dividing line between insanity and calm tempers. Coffee breaks were frequent as the catering area was deemed to be neutral ground in this highly-strung community of talented people.

I was caught up in film fever, so I went to sleep on the grass, as nearly everyone else on the set was doing while the dispute between star and director was thrashed out in the caravans of power.

When the heat became too much I found myself stumbling towards the dining hall in search of refreshment. At least I caught up with my jet-lag, and met a great number of interesting people. One of the assistant directors mistook me for an extra and tried to drag me on to the set. Luckily my protests were heard and, when the poor man discovered what I was there for, I was given a special chair, with fan and umbrella.

Eventually the great star emerged, almost to a hush. I gave him first a bill charged at my full American rate, which he paid nonchalantly, and then we two sat down undisturbed and his reading commenced. It was almost as bizarre as the film he was making. These were the most profitable but exhausting hours I have ever spent.

A lot of clients in New York come to me desperate for a reading. Sometimes I feel that they are over-reacting, but perhaps that is just the New York way.

The strangest client I had was, of all people, a Russian Orthodox archimandrite, the nearest thing their Church has to a bishop. One thing that all strict Christians hold in horror (probably guilt for killing so many of us in the Middle Ages) is psychics of all kinds and descriptions. So you can imagine my utter amazement when this man walked into my apartment in his full religious regalia and asked me for help. Well, I am not going to turn anyone away if they genuinely need my help, and he seemed very straightforward, so off I went, taking my religious client into the heady, etheric realms of the psychic!

Sitting down, my client said to me, 'Mr Lee, I've heard that you're za best predictive psychic in za whole world.'

I had never been called a predictive psychic; it sounded very grand indeed. He told me that he had it by good authority from people in Great Britain and Europe that I was without doubt the best. We got on like a house on fire, and after he visited me a few times, I began to receive other clients from the Russian community, and soon was being offered generous discounts at Russian restaurants all over town. It was as though I had been given an unofficial blessing by this amazing priest.

He consulted me about intricate troubles with his parishes and connected social problems, and about the Russians who had come to him for help in gaining political asylum. Even now he telephones me, wanting to know when I am next coming to the United States, and I receive Christmas cards from him and his assistants. Everyone in his parishes knew that he came to see me, and it was very refreshing to see such honesty in an Orthodox organization like his.

They all paid me handsomely in one way or another.

From the poorer members of the parish I received little money but the most remarkable food parcels, for amongst poor people food means a great deal, and when they share their food with you, they are giving you their trust, respect and something of themselves. Such situations were very touching and these poor Russian Americans had great integrity.

It was slightly ironic that, after taking a doctor as a client, just the once, I then began to receive on a regular basis a string of psychiatrists! Only in New York, I thought to myself. This is psychoanalysis in reverse.

I also did readings for one entire department of the American Broadcasting Corporation, as well as for journalists, and pretty young things from the New York City Ballet. I did a few talk shows on radio and TV in New York, and found that the response was tremendous. Often I was inundated with people wanting to see me. Strangely, I had no cranks. I mean, there must be *some* living in the dark corners of New York.

Central Park was an experience in itself. I used to watch joggers going around the course, and I could sense when one of them was going to have a heart attack. I saved two or three quite by luck, but according to statistics seven people a day would die in Central Park.

Jogging made them prime targets for thieves as well as heart failure. On one occasion a man tried to mug me and take my wallet, but I yelled out at him a favourite British football chant. He took off as fast as he could. He probably thought it was the battle-cry of a weird martial art!

I have some New York friends whom I see on a regular basis, and I would like to tell you about two of them, for they're both highly interesting.

Dennis is a good friend and the chief designer for

164

Cartier in America. He owns a splendid apartment which has become his showpiece. He has a most unusual coffee table; he carved the glass himself, giving it an effect rather like Waterford crystal. He is highly eccentric but very kind, and is completely addicted to Noël Coward. His flat is a strange and shocking blend of antiques and genuine Art Deco. Dennis has a pink 1935 Rolls-Royce which he parks in a garage about four miles away downtown in a security garage safe from car thieves. He uses a taxi in order to use his car!

He is very interested in all things psychic and is very sensitive to the spirit world, and his work is, I feel, directly inspired by the higher forces.

Often Dennis would stride around his flat in a 1930s smoking jacket, smoking an English cigarette at the end of an extremely long and impressive cigarette-holder. It looked more like a blow-pipe than an accessory to sophistication.

When I went to see him, I would find him busily engaged in a sketch, listening to the sombre crooning of Noël Coward. Dennis also has recordings of Noël Coward plays which he knows off by heart. In some vague way, all the frippery and intelligent wit of Coward has inspired him to very serious work for which he has received great acclaim.

He introduced me to some of the wild bohemians of New York's art scene. I was rather sceptical as to how they would relate to a clairvoyant, but I was pleasantly surprised to discover that I was taken very seriously. My reputation had gone before me.

Through Dennis I met the father of pop art, Andy Warhol. The two of us got on well, and the parties that Dennis took me to were always attended by a great many genuine intellectuals, thinkers, philosophers and artists.

At one of these parties I met a woman who also became a client and friend. She is famous in America as a singer-entertainer, and her name is Shirley Gaines. Shirley lives on Riverside Drive and is, without any doubt, the town crier of Manhattan. She is a middle-aged lady, and very beautiful. Often seen playing the piano in a very ritzy nightclub, she is so well known both as a personality and as an artist that Liza Minnelli wrote and sang a song in her honour which became popular all over the world: 'I used to know Shirley of Five Riverside Drive'.

Shirley approaches life with a sonic boom. She is always on the move and she and Dennis help make my brief stays in New York especially happy memorable times.

America has given me a lot of success. The lady in the little café in Amsterdam Avenue, where I used to stumble or stride in for breakfast, depending upon what I had been up to the night before, always knew what I liked. Eggs, sunny side up with pepper. That's my experience of America – with sizzle and a pop, sunny side up, just a touch of pepper!

Chapter 10
Only Twenty-Two Miles from Europe

I love working in Europe. It is only twenty-two miles away across the English Channel. I have flown there many times, but my favourite way to travel to France and beyond is the car ferry from Dover to Calais. I have worked in a number of very different European cities: Amsterdam, Geneva, Paris, Rome, Munich, Düsseldorf. Munich is, apart from Paris, my favourite city, and a good place for me to practise. A lot of prominent people there see me on a regular basis, mainly politicians but also singers from the Bavarian Opera company.

Some of the top German pop stars also come along with their business and personal problems. For a time I retained an apartment in Munich, and it was ideal for entertaining friends and clients.

Musicland, the internationally famous recording studios, is in the Arabella Haus – the complex in which I lived. It is used by groups such as UB40 and, I believe, the Rolling Stones. A lot of famous British bands go there to record. Because of this I have developed good relationships with top names in the music business.

Munich is a startling combination of the old and the new; in my opinion, it is the most magnificent and exciting of all German cities. It far surpasses Berlin, for it is not afflicted with the tensions created by the politics of the Wall. Munich is by and large a happy city. Much of the old royal splendour still remains, with imposing squares where the princes and burghers of times past would congregate. Often I pick up Munich's past as it really was through my psychometry.

The older buildings are striking and beautiful. They make you take notice of the wonderful craftsmanship and artistry that has gone into them. Many of the old buildings have fine examples of figurework, perhaps slightly stiff if compared to their Italian counterparts, but there is an admirable robustness about them.

A lot of the earlier stone figurework dates from the Middle Ages, so intricate it looks as if it could be carved from wood. After the bombardment during the Second World War, the old and the new have been consciously made to reflect the virtues of each other. I used to enjoy walking through the streets: there are many excellent bars with a fine choice of wines or beers. So on any Sunday afternoon in summer or spring, I would enjoy the long walk up the pedestrian mall to my favourite bar in the city centre.

I would stop off at a delicatessen to see a friend of mine, Karl Meyer, who stocked a fine range of tasty morsels. Karl and I had a little ritual: I would give him some psychic advice, and he would give me lunch. This form of barter is how the ancient psychics used to work. It would be nice to receive all one needed by barter.

Karl's wife, Ursula, was a strong, quiet woman, greatly sympathetic to the whole psychic world. Often I would be invited to the flat behind their shop, and after a simple but immaculate dinner Karl, Ursula and I would talk about it. In those enjoyable discussions I found new insights about the psychic realm. Everyone's opinion is important. When I am working day in day out for clients, it is a real boon to have my mind awakened with new ideas that make me reconsider my work and my beliefs.

I find I become energized by cities: they recharge my batteries. My work is *people*, and their needs. A city to me represents hope, the strength of humanity, and the unexpected. European cities seem more relaxed than American ones. I think it is the greater age and the continuing culture. And the very fact that, no matter what the odds have been in the past, ordinary people have rebuilt their lives and have integrated the past into their new way of living.

One aspect of New York I did not like was that ideas, objects, people were all so easily discarded. I think that in Europe and the United Kingdom our sense of history gives us an inborn awareness of just how fragile we humans really are.

I also spent time working in Berlin. It is a sad and dreary place: no one can escape the shadow of the Wall. Its presence and what it represents is everywhere. Much of West Berlin is ultra-modern, rehashed buildings that give off a stark and impersonal feeling. The East German regime is often represented as cruel and harsh, but in the short time I spent in East Berlin I found the people helpful and pleasant, even shy. My psychic abilities went nineteen to the dozen as I tried to pick up the reality behind the scenes. I have done numerous readings there, regardless of the Communist influence, for I was not restricted at all. In fact, I was deluged by people asking me for readings.

In one amazing incident, a man showed me a business card that I had had printed in New York. It had come all the way to London via a friend of his, and then through another friend to East Berlin! This incident is proof of how much my reputation relies on word of mouth, and the ever-helpful assistance of those in the spirit world.

The first time I visited East Berlin, I was a little nervous about the border crossing – all the barbed wire, hungry Alsatian dogs, and machine-guns hidden in strategic positions. I know that everyone must eventually die, but I did not want to end up with my face and shoulders on the Communist side and my rear end pointing towards the face of democracy!

That particular day was rather dark and gloomy and there was a harsh wind blowing. All the grey of the city seemed to take on an ominous gleam. As I walked towards the border post my footsteps seemed to deaden out; there was none of the usual echo. There was no reassuring crowd either, just the steady gaze of the border guards as I made my way to the passport checking office.

The guards stood stiff as if extensions of the severe grey concrete wall behind them. Delicate twirls of barbed wire seemed mournful and sad, as if they were the remains of a rose bush stripped of all its blooms.

The wind sang a plaintive song through the wire, making it vibrate. Rain fell in biting cold drops like a plaintive protest against the division of a once united people. I felt a shiver run through me as if these raindrops were the tears of those who had died trying to escape the East German regime.

Only two days before a young man had been shot as he tried to escape across the Wall to join his girlfriend. She had escaped seven years earlier, proving that love does not see obstacles in barbed wire, concrete, and grey-clad men with machine-guns.

I was touched by this act of heroism, which remained constantly in my mind. When I sensed the earthbound ghost of that poor young man wandering near the passport booth, I prayed quietly that he would find release. As he passed from my vision, I knew that he was going to make one final visit, as spirit, to his lover, so at least in death they would be united. They triumphed in the end.

It was now my turn to present my passport. The guard stared at the passport, a British one, for some time, then at me, and back again at the passport, like watching a game of slow-motion tennis. Eventually he stamped it, and off I went, into the heartland of German Communism.

Once I passed the border patrol, the tension dropped away, and I proceeded to the house where I would do my readings. The people in East Berlin seemed exactly like their Western counterparts. They have the same sort of rollicking humour as West Berliners. It is a spontaneous and open humour, where everyone is included in the joke. They have seen far too much violence and anguish for them to be deliberately cruel. All of them, East and West, want peace and harmony. On both sides of the Wall they sing a traditional song, the 'Berlin Air', that inspires them with images of the city as it was once before it was ravaged by war, and Hitler's madness, and the Wall.

Paris is my largest European practice, and I am glad it is. Besides being a fun place to work, it is always highly exciting, even if you are just sitting by the banks of the Seine watching the world go by. In Paris that is regarded as a worthwhile occupation. Some of France's greatest men were professional dreamers. Paris was the inspiration that made them put their dreams down on paper, in paint, into politics or music, or to be carved out of stone or fused into flowing bronze in a sculptor's forge.

I travel to Paris four times a year, for three weeks at a time. My clients include people from the music world, from classical to jazz, soul, blues, funk, rock, ballads and pop. I also have people from both radio and television journalism, actors, directors, and dancers. So in a way it's similar to New York: mainly top people in the artistic community.

This happened more by accident than design, but I am wondering about that – once again a little help from the spirit world?

A world-famous French film producer and director invited me to Paris at his own expense to do several readings for him and his friends. From the response, this client kindly advertised me by word of mouth and, literally within days, I had hundreds of people in the creative industries coming for guidance.

I even had one very charming elderly lady who came to me with her cat. She wanted to know about the cat's past lives and, when it eventually died, whether it would go to heaven or to hell. This was a tricky one. In the end I refused her money, but bought her lunch at a fashionable restaurant in a first-class hotel, where I explained to her the difference between cats and other animals and human beings when they died, and where they went. I told her that cats did not have individual souls but a group one, and when they died they became part of that group soul again. She was very surprised.

I am always busy in Paris. The moment I am due to leave for the airport I have people begging me for readings, every time. There always seems to be a convoy of passionate Parisians trailing after me, yelling politely over the rumble of traffic for me to do their readings. I usually end up doing last-minute readings at the airport itself. One man got so desperate that he even flew over to Gatwick with me to get a reading done. Once, when I arrived at Gatwick and discovered that I had lost my wallet, I came across a taxi driver who had visited me a few weeks before. He remembered me immediately, and when I told him my plight, he said that he would give me a free lift home if I repaid him with a reading. This I did and he was very happy.

One of the most interesting clients I have in Paris is the pop star Renaud. He has been compared to Bob Dylan for his earthy, enigmatic style and his ability to communicate the vagaries of life in a meaningful way to young people everywhere. His songs have a strong vein of street-wise sentiment, and Paris is the inspiration for his music. In England he was severely criticized in the House of Commons – but by no one else it seemed – for his highly satirical song about Margaret Thatcher. In France it went straight to number one, and remained there for some time.

Renaud was originally a total sceptic, but he became convinced of the reality of the psychic after seeing me for a reading. He even began to refer to the psychic world in his songs, and since that time he has seen me many times, both as friend and client. When he left me the first time, he was, according to onlookers, literally shaking, but half an hour later he returned with a photograph, inscribed *To Peter, who first introduced me to the Supernatural!*

It was such a kind compliment and I have always treasured that photograph. Besides doing predictions for Renaud, I have also done readings for his group and for many of Renaud's close friends. I always claimed to Renaud that he would record an album in an English-speaking country. I psychically knew that this would be America, somewhere in the Los Angeles area, and eventually he would become well known there. Though he has wide appeal, Renaud sings in a very specialized French format, so he did not believe me, and said, 'Peter, you can't be God! You're absolutely and totally wrong. What would the Americans want with my music?' Yet in October 1985 he was making his first recording in Los Angeles.

When I am in Paris I always stay at a hotel opposite Notre Dame. That great cathedral is full of surprises if you study it carefully, for behind the Christian façade you discover all the secret symbols of occult and psychic secret societies. They used Notre Dame to preserve their teachings and knowledge, so every time I go to Paris I spend a few hours learning what I can by reading the vibrations of the place through my psychometry.

The Hotel Esmeralda there is not very well known, but I know the family that runs it extremely well, and, curiously, whenever I telephone to make a reservation, I discover they have already done it! There must be a psychic link!

I go into raptures over French food. To me it is the best in the world. When the French really cook, they make you glad you're hungry!

One senses in Paris the great and sombre parade of history – which is only natural for such an ancient city. The history of Paris seems like some kind of invisible glue that binds all of its various aspects together. Modern buildings as outrageous as the Pompidou Centre mingle in cluttered harmony with old churches and banks. For the Parisians the past is as alive as the present.

I have often walked by the site of the Bastille, that infamous prison of the French Revolution. There I have sensed great bloodshed and horror, a deluge of innocent tears and misery. One almost senses the downward

174

sweep of the guillotine, and psychically I have seen ghostly re-enactments of innocent people being executed there. Within the Bastille, even today, there are many earthbound spirits still in a state of utter shock. Their sudden executions sent them psychically mad.

I came upon one half-mad ghost who implored me for help, for it had begun to realize it was trapped. So I traced a modern-day descendant of this ghostly entity, and revealed to him something in confidence concerning inheritance of money. A day later the spirit reappeared to me, glowing, radiant and free – ready to go towards the light. Something the descendant had done had mysteriously released this innocent victim of the French Revolution, hundreds of years after his death. I was just the go-between.

The most awe-inspiring moment I had in Paris was seeing psychically the faces of a thousand dead soldiers. When I stood by the Arc de Triomphe, and the eternal flame commemorating the unknown warrior, I was over-come with reverence for those countless brave men. For I sensed an almost endless row of marching men, and some kind of low, haunting spirit song. It was as if this great monument was attracting earthbound souls to it as a place of pilgrimage and hope for those in the other world. For a moment, I felt that I the living was intruding on the place of the dead.

Their sacrifice for the liberty of others touched me deeply, and spontaneously a prayer in a wordless language went out from me to the source of creation. And I realized it was not the words of politicians or the signing of treaties that were the factors that stopped wars, but the countless deaths of men and women whose spirits demanded that natural law should put an end to the strife. The implications of that rang like a crystal bell through my mind. Its notes sang out to me the secrets of the spirit world.

Tears streamed down my face – tears for the innocent and naïve sacrifice of countless men and women slaughtered at their masters' bidding. Sensing the enormity of what I had experienced, I sat down on a bench and lit a cigarette. As I smoked, I watched the blue smoke drift, spirit-like, over the rooftops of Paris. The world around me had changed. The colours were brighter and more alive; my psychic abilities had expanded.

I thanked God for my abilities. Slowly I got up and began to walk down the avenue. It was the longest walk I had ever taken in my life. Every person that I passed, I was at one with. Every tree and flower and its perfume was like a new thing just created. The moment sparkled and sounded with one single word that only the soul can hear.

I took my time, wandering at leisure, then met some friends, as arranged, and spent the night at a cabaret, where heaven and hell faded into nothingness as creation shed its light all over me. The taste of my cocktail was never better. The conversation of my friends united us in happiness and every ordinary little thing seemed divine. I had plucked a fermented grape from the vine of harmony and drunk its wine.

The Arc de Triomphe became to me a symbol of spiritual renewal, and a triumph of the divine being ordinary. The secret to harmony.

Just as I ordered my second cocktail, these two sayings came out of nowhere, as if people from the spirit world were whispering them to me. Everything around me was silent as a gentle voice said, '*When the outside becomes the inside, then truly the Kingdom of Heaven is come.*'

I took out my ballpoint pen and began to scribble on

a paper napkin, rather absentmindedly. As I looked down at what I had done, I was surprised to read, '*There is the World behind the World.*' And I laughed. All my life I had been in search of the mystical and the miraculous. Now it had found me – the great indescribable! I bought my friends a round of drinks and together we celebrated Life.

Later that night I made my way home to the hotel. The street outside was quiet except for a man whistling beautifully some love song. I didn't know its name, but I knew the tune, and it sparked off the whole experience again, so I wrote down this poem, and I'd like to share it with you.

Meditation On Life

There are a thousand voices calling,
songs of spirit, in silent praise,
words of wisdom,
born from pain, and I have come,
innocent and alone, here before
this tragic stone.
I hear triumph, there is
triumph in death, for behind
this world, there is another world,
born, born, born out of
creation's single breath!

Chapter 11

How Clairvoyance Works

Many of my clients are mystified how I foretell their futures in such a forthright and accurate manner. They are amazed, as often I am (even after all my years of experience), that I am hardly ever wrong. I'm never wrong on very important issues.

Often, out of innocent curiosity, I have been asked how I see the future, discover revelations of the past, pierce the veil of the elusive present and unlock the atom of the moment. Now is the time to explain just how I do predict the fate of nations, governments, the rich, the famous, the ordinary, of the world and its tentative future.

Because I am clairvoyant I am able to predict the future in many different ways. By 'seeing' psychically – which is clairvoyance; 'hearing' psychically – which is clairaudience; and through psychometry – divination from the vibrations of an object. I become 'sensitive' with all the previous experiences of my client, which then in turn, through an intricate process of cause and effect based on natural law, enables me to see the future. I do not see the future with the human eye, but with the ever-present eye of the spirit. The spirit is beyond all comprehension of time, human logic, space and anything that can be comprehended in an empirical way. Clairvoyance is a paralogical art beyond the limits of logic. It is without any doubt at all a parapsychology which defies the limits in which we normally see the world. The psychic expresses itself in many varying forms. Primarily and essentially it is another but more complex aspect of the subconscious and unconscious mind interacting under the wealth of information that comes to us from everyday experiences.

The ability to predict events on the world scene comes from reading the mind of humanity. That we have a group identity, that we are one species, is the fountainhead of how the psychic is most easily translated into the material world through receivers – commonly known as mediums or clairvoyants.

I feel that psychics work through this means far more in prediction than do mediums, who work with those in the spirit world, just one level up from the earth plane. Modern psycho-physical scientists have come to recognize that the group mind of humanity does exist. It's a crying shame that it has taken so long for the narrow-minded amongst us to realize this. The teaching of the Hindus, Guatama Buddha and the great masters of the Western mystery and magical traditions, all expressed the same reality and experience of the group mind – that particular and peculiar energy that makes us human.

One of the least attractive aspects of my work is the deeper sensitivity I have to pain than most people. Often, when I predict unpleasant things or disasters, I find that I experience the suffering of that event. Through this I have learnt how suffering and pain can be avoided. A psychic like me can predict the future because something is *going to* happen. By tuning in I can interpret the information and relay it in a sensible and orderly message. It is rather like a fisherman sitting on a river bank and, having placed his line into the fast-moving river, calmly waiting for a bite from the fish in the depths below. Therefore I have cast my line into the psychic river in the direction of prediction and prophecy, in order to obtain the information essential to help others. It is far easier, though, if I have a target to cast my line at – a person or object from which to gain information through its vibrations.

At other times the higher forces give me information that hits me like a flash, and usually works for the benefit of everyone. Then I am prompted by the very importance of the message I have received to act on it.

When I do readings for clients, I see for each of them a definite occurrence of events. Things that *will happen*. I seldom deal in 'maybe'. Sometimes I do have a client for whom there is, for some reason, more than one pathway open in the reading. Situations of firmly mapped destiny are far more common than split-destiny situations, but when this latter does happen, I find that careful emphasis must be placed on explaining the importance of having two paths from which to choose, and why a client should be totally sure of the choice made, for once chosen, the die is cast. Split-destiny situations are usually related to a major change in attitude or lifestyle that has come from a former life.

Often predictions appear to me in a three-dimensional way, rather like a waking dream. Of course, I am often guided myself in this way. Like most people, I get warning or informative dreams that help me. Dreams are very important, and they should never be ignored or dismissed but interpreted with intelligence. For it is in the dream state and the sleep state that the higher forces can reveal knowledge to us. Also, in a state of complete solitude it becomes a great deal easier for the higher forces to have a chat with us. Silence and time on one's own helps to heighten one's sensitivities and can teach us to sort out the true psychic communications with higher forces from the garbage of everyday existence that rattles around in everyone's head.

When I'm in the dream state, ready for prediction, I see these 'dreams' as a three-dimensional vision. Yet the term 'dream' is not exactly right; it is more as though I am taking part in the event while at the same time watching myself in the vision. A good illustration of that is when I helped save Dr Umaro Dikko's life.

At other times my psychic experience is just a very heightened sense of 'knowing', as if the future is falling into my hands on behalf of my client – which is in fact what happens. In this extreme sense of knowing, all my physical and psychic senses are merged in harmony with each other to work as one integrated unit. It is through this combination and blending that the sixth sense is formed and I can give out the required information to eager clients.

When I work with a client to give a reading, I find it an added advantage to use psychometry although it's not always needed. Psychometry is the holding of an object which, because it belongs to somebody or has been on somebody's person, retains the vibration of that person. Those vibrations contain the actions or *life* of that person, past, present and future. This means that I am able to do readings for people even if they are not present. When the person is present, it needs a slightly lesser form of psychometry, for the client is also giving off vibrations to me, as is the object. The object then enhances the strength of the reading. Thus it acts as a link between me and my client.

To understand psychometry better, we can take the example of a record. The sound in the grooves is not somebody's voice, but the reproduction of somebody's voice. In the same way an object retains the vibrations of the owner.

I do not always use psychometry in my readings, but in certain cases it is the best technique for the situation.

The psychic energies speak to me in a soft, gentle language which is not of this earth plane. This language is well known to me and other genuine psychics: it is a language of light and sound. In my own simple way I translate this into whatever language I am speaking, whether German or English. A psychic in the heart of the Amazon jungle hears the same psychic language, but then translates it into his or her native tongue. The psychic language therefore is universal. It is the language of wisdom, power and joy that issues from the very heart of creation itself. Coming back to a definition of this psychic language, the closest I can come to describe it is as a very high-frequency communication. A soundless sound. A lightless light. The matrix of consciousness.

This psychic language is an all-knowing, on-going moment – as if the universe itself had paused to gather its breath. When I use this psychic language, or music of the spheres as it is sometimes called, I find that I withdraw from time as it is commonly understood, and only very powerful natural psychics or mediums can do this. From this withdrawal come great and soul-shaking predictions. It is as though I am looking down on time and motion, seeing all the aspects of material reality from the static position of eternity. But even in that state I am far from the source of creation itself.

To illustrate this point further, it is as if I was in space, looking down on the earth and seeing everything – man, woman, child, animal, plant, amoeba, nuclear missile, the hanky-panky in Cabinet rooms – all of it in microscopic detail.

*

How do you approach a psychic and get your money's worth, especially if you are going for the first time? Approach them without fear and with careful scrutiny. Even in times of need, use your intuition to aid you in the choice you make. The size of their fee does not always indicate the ability of the psychic. Take that into consideration. Go by how you feel about the psychic as a person. Be selective, depending on what you want. It would be a waste of time and money to go to a medium if you needed a prediction about the future, just as it would be a total waste of time and money if you came to a clairvoyant expecting to hear a message from your Uncle Albert who had recently died.

If, for example, you are going to see a psychic just to experiment, which is OK, give the young psychics a chance. Go and see a few of them. But you may instead have a really valid and important reason to see a psychic. If so, go to someone with a rock-solid reputation. Check them out. Every good psychic has a widespread reputation.

Remember that psychics only get good reputations if their work is excellent. And excellence is not magically bestowed upon them, as people would have us believe. It takes years of hard work, and if you are fated to work as a psychic, you go through hell at first in order to know your craft. Suffering often deepens sensitivity – but not always. It is always preferable to select a psychic who is not locked into any particular religious belief or dogma. Otherwise you will get only a partial message, coloured by his or her own beliefs and attitudes. The best psychics are humanist in feeling and action. So try to find a free-flowing mind, someone who is in contact with the light of the Godhead without the trappings and will not preach at you, or try to convert you. There is nothing worse than a psychic who preaches when all the client needs is a straightforward and concise prediction.

It is important that the psychic you choose should also be worldly wise, and usually the really good ones are. Often they go to extremes, but then we are all human. Don't judge a psychic by what you can see of his private life, if anything. If you can find a psychic with all these qualities, still realize that you do not have to accept what he says. But what he says is likely to be accurate and useful.

So then, listen to him! Let him be free to tell you not just about what will be in the future, but also and importantly what is bothering you now – what the underlying problem is, in other words – and why. Let him tell you about your past, to prove that you as a paying client can rely on his psychic skills. And, if he does this in a helpful manner, then on the whole (no psychic is God!) he is going to be right.

Even though he may tell you truths that you just do not want to hear, it is because he really does want to help you. Harsh words may hide a gentle heart.

A responsible psychic can help you prepare for the good times as well as the bad. Going to a psychic is not all crystal balls, joss sticks and misery, as some people imagine. Let a psychic help you to understand why things are the way they are, and, if you feel confident, any prediction made will happen as you were told it would – and you will be able to deal with the situation.

Going to a psychic is a very personal thing. I do sincerely believe that some psychics suit some people better than others. It is very much about how person-alities react together, how psychic and client tune in to each other. The client is the final judge of any psychic, and how the prediction relates to his or her own need.

I do not in any way advocate that people should go

running to their favourite psychic every five minutes over the slightest problem. I tell people, after I have given them a reading, to come back to me when they feel that they may really need me, whether it be in five minutes, five years, or fifteen years. When they return is up to them; it has nothing to do with me. I am there for genuine problem-solving only, and for accurate and honest predictions.

Sometimes I do readings about people's past lives. When I state consciously that I wish to go into their past lives, then I receive in visual form a story and/or a commentary with a voice telling me all the information. In fact, the voice rather resembles Michael Caine's. I wonder if he knows something I do not! Then I am told the reason why they departed their last life, and any major or dramatic events that took place particularly related to their present life. So I tune in to the past life to find answers to the present question. It can often be very revealing and of great use.

The past contains the future. I believe and accept the transmigration of souls, and from past lives things that we need to learn come through with us into this life. A soul will return, or migrate, from one life to another – rather like a winged seed on a spring wind – on its eventual journey to the Godhead, or whatever name you would like to tack on to the force beyond comprehension.

The soul migrates through time, for it is trapped within time until its final liberation. Time is indeed parallel. Time and life occur at one and the same endless eternal moment. But this goes beyond description. All of this is part of the fabric of prediction. People reincarnate first and foremost to learn lessons that can only be achieved on this plane of reality. Often we may learn our lessons in an easier way by re-enacting events which have taken place in previous lives.

Often souls reincarnate due to a great attraction to a loved one in the previous life, or someone they are called back to help in some way – or even, but rarely, to help the world evolve one stage up, if the soul is advanced enough. Karma, or the cause and effect of the universal law which creates our destiny, draws us back to the earth in order to learn our lesson. For example, the great musicians return partly to achieve more for themselves, but also to give others uplifting pleasure. Through their music, the mysteries of life become better known.

Then there is another example, at the other end of the human scale, but closely connected, and that is the mentally and physically handicapped people of the world. Some of these handicaps are caused by accident, not by karma, for karma is pliable like any other energy within the material world. When a serious accident takes place, usually death follows, and a new start sparks into life. Karma often is indirectly misused, and a prime example is the children born deformed by drugs. It is a frightening thought to most people that we could well return to earth only to be trapped as a handicapped person. For some hidden reason known only to the soul concerned, it would be directly related to an event in a previous life. Perhaps for inflicting unbearable pain upon someone else in that previous existence – so as to make the soul concerned take stock of what pain and frustration are. The justice of natural law is impartial and uncompromising. We usually return because we have not achieved all that we can or should, or what we have to say or do in the world, until we live our life as best we can and share it to enrich other people's lives.

As I understand it, the reason for living is to become in true touch with the energy of Life. Psychically, I feel that we should integrate and harmonize with nature, the world, and especially with each other, and the foundation of all: the creative force. The whole purpose of us being here is to become with ease part and parcel of creation. The creation that somehow we, for want of a more accurate word, have 'rebelled' against.

Often, when people come to me for predictions, I find myself in the role of the comforter, teacher, advisor, or healer. I am there for the enlightenment of the client, or for the clarification of a situation which perplexes the client. It varies greatly. Often I can be used by the spirit forces to stimulate a client's interest in high realities, but that is quite rare. There are times when clients have great pain, psychic or emotional and, sometimes, physical. I try to heal these people through prediction. Prediction is a healing tool. Often in healing people, I cleanse them of their pain by closing down my other senses and willing all my psychic force into them. The ability of being able to experience the same things as my client adds to the power of healing. I have been forced to do this in order to learn to be aware of other people's feelings, and often life kicks me up the backside and sends me on little refresher courses of experience. Also when doing readings I gain a great deal of information from my own past lives.

As far as my own past lives are concerned, I use the information that I discover to give me greater understanding about the lessons that I have to learn. We are here to learn. If we had nothing more to learn, we would not be here on earth! Past lives teach us that life goes on, that the spirit does not die; man is eternal spirit.

Humanity would progress much faster if we as a

species, as a multitude of races, as a chaotic inter-mingling of cultures, had no extremes of any kind; just the awareness of the vibrant, middle path of balance that nature achieves without ever having to have learnt it. So no extremes. No monks. No nuns. No Yorkshire Rippers or madmen nicknamed Jack. No rapists – nothing like that. Just the middle path: no sex-fiends, no celibates. There is a natural pathway of balance based on reason, sharing and respect. We should be as the natural law demands us to be. So if you're gay, be gay but happy. If you're heterosexual, be heterosexual but not straight-laced. If you're bisexual, be bisexual but not a split personality. If you're a cow, moo! If you're a dog, bark, don't try to meow! If you're a human being, act like one! For a moment, examine the term. Human being equals being human. But harm no one in being what you are. Then the middle path is discovered.

Chapter 12
Predicting the Future of Mankind

Now I would like to make a few predictions about forthcoming world events and how they will change the destiny of the human race. Some may not seem particularly earth-shattering, but if you study them you will discover that the effects upon the world will indeed be far-reaching. Can anyone imagine England without the royal family? An interesting idea?

These predictions may help to wake people up to the fact that they can change the destiny of the world for the better. Let us first look at Great Britain in the 1990s, a period when the entire future of the world is going to go through major change. Some of it is far from pleasant.

Great Britain

I feel that Great Britain will make steady progress from the year 1987 until 1989. There is, however, regardless of the prosperity engendered in the period between those years, a major testing point in 1990. This will be directly related to shaky world events and a major crisis that will shock the world. There will be a fearful situation hanging over Britain. There will be civic unrest with riots and violence. But Britain will pull through. There may be a thorn in its side due to a major rift in

Northern Ireland that could banish the British association with Northern Ireland.

The following seven years for Britain and the world generally will be of intense importance, for in 1997 a great period of danger could throw the world into panic. A new world war could start like wildfire. This depends, however, on the relationships between East and West by that time. Britain could move into the forefront of the political arena concerning this problem. There will be, strangely, a boom time from 1990 until 1997 for British industry and the country as a whole. There will be a re-emergence of British military influence on the world scene, with the balance of power changing dramatically in Europe.

During this time, there is going to be a great turn-around in the British monarchy. A monarch will reign, but for a short time. A sudden tragedy will end the rule. This will be followed by a short and extremely tempestuous regency which will encourage a fast-growing and negative attitude towards British royalty in the international community. This will spell out very quickly the last days of royalty. *The last reigning monarch will be one of Prince Charles's sons*. He will reign for a very short time and I feel that Prince Andrew will be forced into a regency. Britain will find itself under a dramatically changed system of government: a republic of intense and possibly extreme political ideas, at first.

Then it will become very middle-of-the-road. There will be no major disaster of any great effect, and war on any large scale will turn out to be a storm in a Wedgwood teacup.

At this point, my deepest and sincerest belief is that *unless choice and the understanding of how our future may develop unite to change the end result, there will follow two nuclear wars*. One will be extremely quick, lasting only a few days, but incredibly devastating. It will be in the Middle East. It will come as far as Eastern Europe, perhaps, and could even spread as far as the Rhine. The second, and this will be before this century is out, will follow ten to twelve years after the first. But this will only happen if those in power haven't learnt their lesson by then. These wars will only take place if people do not find solutions to peace, and do not unite through what they have in common, rather than argue over their differences. To argue is to bring disaster!

If there is to be no agreement to peace, if nothing is worked out that can be used as a tangible device to unite the world, then this second nuclear war will bring this planet, this small planet of ours, the fragile earth, close to almost total destruction. There will be great misery. Ash will be everywhere from the incinerated remains of populous cities. Human wrecks will wander the streets before dying in agony from radiation sickness and horrific flash burns. Hell will have come to stay! There will be a few people left who will survive and start again. *But I feel that in the year two thousand three hundred, there is a great possibility that the world will cease.* It will go into its own black hole, so to speak, and be regenerated over thousands and thousands of years. Like every other soul, every other living thing, the earth will need a great deal of time to replenish and grow again. This prediction of mine comes into conflict with that of Nostradamus. But I feel that he was unduly pessimistic about the world's end, and out by three hundred years.

Once again it must be said that unless people in power sit down to create resolutions for peace, there will be no tomorrow. The last summit between Reagan and Gorbachov is a small but essential start to peace and the aversion of catastrophe. Unless more is done on a regular basis, psychically I see a cold war of massive proportions between the two superpowers. Psychically I feel that the Americans should take incredible care in the choice of their next president, otherwise on the ticket of avid nationalism, spurred on by the belief of American supremacy and, possibly, racial superiority, a warmonger who shows one face to his nation and another to the world will be placed into a position of power. He will be difficult to remove from office. The world will recoil at his bite. His own nation will bemoan their fate!

I predict that the monetary system and the economics of the West will collapse entirely before the year two thousand and ten. A totally new system of exchange will be developed. Gold will not be used as the base ever again. The East will feel, in fact, that this will be their big chance, but because of the close liaisons between the financial institutions of the world, the East's financial system will also bite the dust. Depending upon the leaders who come to power in order to sort out this problem, either peace or great conflict will be the outcome. I can tell you that if every man, woman and child were to go out and buy a candle, light it and dedicate it totally to peace for just one moment, there would by the power of their pleas be world peace for ever.

South Africa: The Countdown Has Begun!

The final countdown has begun. South Africa as we all know it is on the brink of collapse. So this brings me to that eyesore of the twentieth century. A festering wound under the guise of democracy. The wound is South Africa. Psychically I see that *unless the South African government releases Nelson Mandela from prison, they will have a huge organized bloodbath, far worse than any previous violence, and the white minority will be, literally, pushed into the sea.* It will be greater than if Mandela was free and organizing it. Both blacks and whites, young and old, will be involved in full-scale revolution. Unless the South African government hands power over to a transitional regime based on the example of Zimbabwe, then the government will perish, and the stability of Africa and the Western world will be in doubt. Huge outpourings of violence could sweep up through the African continent because of the great unrest in South Africa.

Out of this valley of blood there is going to rise up an African Joan of Arc. It will not be any of the immediate leaders, but the daughter of Nelson and Winnie Mandela. This young woman will have hate, born of misery and suffering caused to her people, as the main weapon with which she will activate and awaken huge followings of black and white people in South Africa. There will be even more violence; she shall decimate the last vestiges of white South African rule. She will be inspired by her hate to wipe out and destroy. She will not talk. The wisdom of Zimbabwe's Robert Mugabe concerning this problem will not be there and the influence of other black leaders will be ignored, with some being put to the sword by her. Her great mass of followers will sweep across South Africa like a plague

193

of locusts. She may die in one of the skirmishes, days before South Africa is finally the country of the black majority. The souls of those massacred under apartheid will be savagely avenged.

Actions for peace must be implemented before it is far too late for talk.

South Africa's incursions into neighbouring countries may quickly create a situation where several black African countries combine forces, declaring war on South Africa!

If this does happen, as I feel that it could, South Africa will be out on a limb, and hardly any country within the international community will come to its aid. The biggest problem is that after the white government is vanquished, certain superpowers may try to move in and lay a large claim to the huge wealth of South Africa, as well as gaining political and military footholds.

So it may be some time after the black people have regained South Africa as their rightful homeland that they will be able to live and enjoy their country's riches free from foreign interference.

Other Trouble Spots

In South America, Chile will go through a major and catastrophic revolution unless the corruption is removed entirely from the government and its associate concerns. This will also ignite tension in other South American countries. The United States may intervene, but actually serve in making the situation worse. The United States of America may also suffer horribly from disasters due to natural law bringing down justice on the US for its covert influence in violence in other parts of the world. Many innocent people in the US will lose their lives in earthquakes and tidal waves.

I feel, psychically, that the peoples of the southern hemisphere will be placed in the hard and difficult position of peacemakers, and already Australia, emerging as a major South-East Asian and Pacific power, and New Zealand, the voice of conscience, are leading the way against nuclear armament and deployment. They can become a great force for peace, because countries like Japan need the influence of peacemakers. I sense that Japan may soon change a lot of its political alignments with other countries as internal turmoil begins to get out of control. In Japan, a rising military influence is on the horizon.

The young people of today, who in reality are far more peaceful than those of my generation, are the ones who will finally influence the way things turn out. If we allow these two nuclear wars actually to happen, there will evolve a new generation of what could be termed 'the new people'. They will possess psychic gifts in abundance and they will come to the forefront to bring new and inspired guidance. The old ideas of leadership will no longer apply. They will cause people, by example, to live in harmony and peace. To be in harmony with nature will be the known but unspoken law. Humanity will be filled with a 'divine common sense'. This will be the nearest thing to the Biblical Second Coming of a great spiritual being. There will be no individual but many, all with one purpose: harmony. This will take place whether we avoid nuclear war or not.

If we avoid war, then we are taking the first real steps towards an integrated and harmonious world. If we don't, the power-seekers will rise up again. In the more harmonious situation, the power-seekers will try to take control again, but they will be without much influence, and those with wisdom will say that natural law unfortunately demands the death of such people. The power-seekers will be exterminated by injection. It is a chilling concept for a society to be based on . . .

They will be put down, and regarded by people everywhere as very dangerous low forms of life. No longer would anyone be believed to threaten the peace and harmony of the world at large or its member nations.

As regards the nuclear fall-out from the Middle Eastern atomic war, the population of Europe will react in total panic. The Western governments will behave in a very brutal manner. Almost fascist. It will be the survival of the élite.

The Unification of Europe: The United States of Europe

Great Britain as a nation must learn how to integrate with other cultures and other countries. Britain will merge the best it has with that of the countries in Europe, and this, I feel, will form the United States of Europe.

France and the United Kingdom will resolve any problems they might have, enabling this unified Europe to act for the improvement of the world. The United States of Europe will become a major decision-maker in the international affairs of the world.

By Europe uniting the best qualities of each country, major steps will be taken towards peace that will embrace the entire world. For example, if a German girl takes a Chinese man in marriage, she doesn't cease to be German or he Chinese, but they share a harmony based upon what each other gives. It can be the same, but on a far more complex scale, of course, unifying the nations of the world, with Europe as the first example.

*

But these few predictions that I have made are all in the future. I made them expressly so that we all can be aware that we can shape our future in a far more constructive way. No one in their right mind wants war if they know that they are going to die, and that all they hold dear will perish along with them; even those who start wars want peace of some kind. Everyone deep inside wants peace and harmony. So it is far more important to concentrate upon making today peaceful so that the next day will be as well. Create peace for the moment and it will create peace of its own accord. Peace gives birth to peace. What we all want is a natural birth of peace and harmony. Therefore we must learn that it is important that what you do now in your day-to-day life creates a balance on the fulcrum of the future. Your hand, as is my hand, is the one hand that decides whether it is destiny by button and bomb, or destiny by choice of communication created through caring for one's fellow human being, on this our only planet.

This planet we call Earth because that is what is under our feet! The earth grows our food; wouldn't it be good to see it as it is now, rather than dry dustbowls where once green grassland grew? Or forests, majestic and beautiful, instead of charred dusty barren waste-lands? Beautiful city parks, not petrified tangles of human life covered over by copious amounts of grey ash blown all over the once gentle face of the earth by a radioactive wind? The choice is yours. Without brotherhood, without sisterhood, without humanity becoming responsible for itself, there will be no peace.

I sincerely hope my predictions of destruction do not come true.

*

As we are talking about prediction I would really like to share with you a most marvellous experience that I had on 29 December 1984. I was invited to the television breakfast chat show, 'Good Morning Britain'. Henry Kelly, the television presenter, was very interested in talking to me about what might happen in the coming year, 1985. Henry is a very nice man, and to be fair he had invited two other psychics to the show in order to gain different opinions about what the future held for Britain, Europe and the world at large.

I had been to a rip-roaring party put on the night before by some showbusiness associates. I arrived at the studio in a state of gallant disrepair. But I was truly amazed at how quickly the psychic energies within began to fill me, revitalize me and put me in touch with some very relevant and quite literally earth-shaking predictions for the year that was to burst upon us. But for all the good intentions of my psychic associates, I felt that I was the only one, for some reason, who said anything of any real value. I predicted things that actually happened during the course of 1985. Of course, my associates were both well-known and responsible psychics who have reputations built on accuracy and integrity, but in that particular situation the spirit spoke through me.

Henry introduced me and my associates to the breakfast-time audience and then asked me a few questions.

'Peter, you are a clairvoyant?'

'Yes, that's right, Henry,' I said in a most serious tone, trying to stifle a yawn at the same time.

'Tell me, with your international reputation, I suppose you can tell me this. What does a clairvoyant actually do?' Henry was genuinely interested.

I replied quite simply, 'Well, in my case, as in many

others, a clairvoyant predicts the past, the present and the future for people. That's it in a nutshell, Henry.'

He looked at me and then smiled a mischievous smile. 'Tell me, Peter, what does 1985 hold for the world?'

'For the world, now let me see,' I said, interested at what was going to pop out of me at that time of the morning.

Henry butted in. 'Will it end?' he said dryly.

'No, Henry, I can assure you and the audience, not in 1985 and not for a long time to come.'

'Will 1985 be full of natural disasters, Peter?' he asked, once again concerned.

'Will it be full of natural disasters? Let me see. I don't feel so many natural disasters in the world at once, but I do feel that we are going to see and have on our hands a very serious earthquake in 1985. Possibly two within the same geographical area.'

I paused for a moment, and then continued. 'On the political scene, however, there will be a lot of changes in 1985, particularly related to the Kremlin, in the structure of power especially. This will change the obvious political scene, as well as the scene behind the public image. It feels as if Soviet politics will go through a major public relations change. This will give greater impetus to the East-West dialogue and therefore East-West relations are going to better themselves very much. But I do feel that there is going to be a serious row in early 1985 between the United States of America and the Soviet Union.'

Then suddenly I felt impelled to tell Henry as talk had drifted on to the British royal family that Prince Andrew would be involved in a scandal in 1985.

That particular television appearance that I did served to be a good document to the validity and accuracy of psychic prediction. In relation to my prediction about the Kremlin I also mentioned that there would be deaths within the Kremlin. There was the death of Andropov, a major event that placed Gorbachov in the path to supreme power within the Soviet Union. Then there was the tragic earthquake in Mexico City and huge mudslides in Colombia, which galvanized the world community into sympathy and compassion.

On less serious matters, in the London *Standard* of Monday, 6 January 1986, I did a series of predictions for famous rock stars. I would like to share these with you, and then together we shall see these things happen as I have predicted.

In the coming months of 1986, Elton John, Mick Jagger, forever a Rolling Stone, and the king of fast music with style, Michael Jackson, are all going to have a rough ride ahead, sad to say. I feel that Michael is going to be involved in some form of scare or terrible event which will create for him a psychic wound of intense proportions. And poor old Elton John's marriage will be in dire straits. Mick Jagger may have to cease his frolics, especially when he dances in the street at all hours, because his health may suffer. He has to be careful with it.

I would also like to make a prediction for that ever-popular crowd-pulling band, Wham! I do feel that there may be trouble ahead for them in the legal sense with some person taking a great deal of money off them, and one of them is going to make a very brave announcement to the world at large about a very personal matter.

Chapter 13
Impressions from Another World

No, this chapter isn't about Mike Yarwood, that extremely talented impressionist! First of all, my own impressions from the deep well of my psychic subconscious come from many other worlds. Not just from the many esoteric or higher psychic worlds of spirit, as well as those below this one, but also from other planets. Often when I am doing readings I find that I come across indications of life forms from different worlds.

I am totally convinced in all seriousness that the earth has had visitations from beings from other planets over many thousands and thousands of years, as well as now. I also feel that some of them have interbred with humanity. I feel that they, rather like birdwatchers or naturalists, are keeping an eye on things very carefully. They wish us to keep our world intact, and not endanger the rest of the galaxy. They are doing this for their own safety as well.

Some years ago I was asked to unravel a truly extra-terrestrial mystery. Someone from the University of Queensland in Australia asked me to use my psychometry to find out the truth concerning some ancient 'stones' that were in a crater in Queensland. They were two different colours: one a silver-ashen grey, the other a deep and vibrant blood-red. In a semi-trance, I related to a tape recorder, for the results were to be sent back to Australia, that the grey objects were not stones at all, but some kind of metal that had been fossilized, petrified. The red stone, also in a petrified state, was a component of an energy machine of some sort. When brought under scientific investigation they had no relationship to any other kind of stone or petrified or fossilized object on earth. There was no comparison. Nothing was similar.

The conclusion I came to – with the higher forms and forces speaking through me – was that the 'stones' belonged to another civilization that had settled for some length of time in Australia many many thousands of years ago! I saw how they lived. They dwelt in great domes, hundreds of kilometres wide, high, almost glasslike in appearance. And in these domes, they went out into the world on all types of expeditions. They visited all parts of the world, contributing to the advance of the human race, as others had done in the early stages of their evolution.

Their visit to the earth was fact-finding and exploratory. They helped the cultures already in progress to become more stable. They also interbred purposely, and then, eventually, they went away back to their homes. Their own planet. The earth was not their natural environment. These beings that I saw resembled human beings as we are today, similar in structure and bone formation although their skin was slightly different.

Of course, in those days, human beings were different: rather apish and deformed-looking. Qualities we still retain in our minds!

These same beings still visit us today. Some are here with amnesia, as we have voluntary amnesia when we reincarnate. Some come here knowing full well who they are, for a purpose known only to them. Proof exists. It is well documented. It will not be long before we come to terms with this and regard it as a natural occurrence, but it will be quite some time before the world at large meets these beings from outer space on a face-to-face basis.

But the space people await in eagerness the day when mankind can sit down and have afternoon tea with them, so to speak.

Another interesting point about these visitations is that they normally occur over sacred sites, monuments or places of ancient worship. It is also interesting to note that governments have an alarming but regular tendency to hide and build secret weapon installations over these sacred sites. Think about it; why does this happen? I feel that before we destroy each other, in order to protect themselves and others, there may be some form of attempted intervention from those in space.

But I feel they won't be very successful. So, once again, the warning comes back: we have to save ourselves, on our own. No space messiah is going to be able to do it for us. With our destructive minds and tendencies, we would probably try to destroy our space friends before they had a chance to speak to us!

Now I would like to share with you my experience of the higher and lower planes of reality, and how I get impressions that enable me to predict. All the planes of existence, including the earth plane, are pointing towards the one indefinable, but unifying and harmonious, timeless and motionless enlightenment.

I receive impressions of these other worlds through readings and prediction, and through other psychics, soothsayers and prophets. Since man first learnt to communicate and share ideas, philosophers have tried to talk about these other worlds and their eventual journey to the Absolute.

My spiritual guides have also imprinted these impressions in my mind, to make me realize the spirit does not die, and that life is a continuous voyage which changes its shape every now and then, usually when it is time to reincarnate. It is best to be at peace to ask questions about other realities, and when I have been at peace, I have received answers along these lines.

Humanity stands, as I far as I am able to understand, at a crossroads. One plane of reality may hold a thousand planes of reality all interwoven; one stage in that reality, a thousand stages. Everything in eternity, which includes our world, is like the spinning of a spider's web. All is one piece, intermingling, united by one mysterious bond. Every action, wish or thought is a component of this web.

The more intelligent we are, the greater number of webs we spin. And this is what we call our karma, or cause and effect. The energy of destiny. The cut and parry of fate. These webs all join up somehow.

But now let us move on to individual planes of existence, and discover what they are all about. Now I sincerely believe that we exist here on earth in a fairly primitive state, in what I would call the positive-negative plane. This does not mean that it is the first plane of existence, but I am convinced that below the earth plane in which we live, on a psychic and different material reality (due to its vibrational rate), there is a totally negative plane. The way of existence is designed so that those beings who inhabit it are working out the destiny of that plane and themselves by being totally negative, even evil and malicious!

This may sound like something from the Middle

Ages. Hellfire and brimstone! Devils tossing poor damned souls into lakes of boiling metal! It's not like that. So let me explain further. On this earth plane we are on the whole, as human beings, both positive and negative, or, simply put, good and bad, pessimistic or optimistic – a blend of both. We have a choice between positive and negative actions, thoughts or ideas. In the negative plane, that is not the case. There is no choice. The concept of being positive does not exist.

So on this negative plane there exist spirit forms, or 'people' for ease of description. We all began as spirit 'germs', so to speak, just as a flower grows, or a tree grows. These negative spirit forces are quite happy to be negative, because that is their way. For example, if an atom was reversed or inverted, it would split the world asunder. It would implode. Those who dwell in this doubly negative plane are completely the reverse of us. However, there are human beings who through total wretchedness, instead of progressing to the next plane, higher or complementary, fall into this negative plane I have just described. I must firmly stress that very few human beings ever enter into this state of abject and depraved existence. I have observed this plane through intense states of clairvoyance. These poor souls would have to work very hard, very hard indeed, in ultimate misery, in order to get back on to something like the earth plane. And, for the length of time they would have to work, it would be comparable to our conception of eternity.

They are within a prison of time and space, unable to break free. Time has fenced them in. Yet, because there is in reality no punishment as in the concept of a wrathful or personal God – only natural law – they are not bound for ever and ever. They have the chance to progress. There is an old saying that comes from the

205

ancient mystery schools of Western Europe which may help to explain it further: 'For every cell within your body there is a life. For every cell that dies, there is a death.'

In other words, there is a constant renewal going on, and it seems as though it lasts for ever. Therefore when souls go to this negative plane, they take the thoughts they had in the earth plane – and thus they bring all their cunning, craftiness and misery with them. Sometimes they can sneak back into the earth plane. They can wait for the right kind of conception, usually with stressful circumstances of an extreme kind surrounding a young mother. They nip in, grow into a foetus, a baby which is then born. Then they wreak havoc upon an unsuspecting neighbourhood, city, country, or the entire world, depending upon their force. Because they are not ready for responsible reincarnation on the earth or even for conducting themselves in association with human beings, the end result is a totally negative, confused and powerful personality. Sometimes fate is kind to them. They die early or end up under lock and key in a psychiatric hospital, away from the world.

Evil is a good word for describing such people. But once again I must stress that they are few and far between. Perhaps Adolf Hitler was one of these. Perhaps, even though some may scoff, Julius Caesar! If you ever, which I hope you don't, come across such beings, then you are quite justified in refusing them help of any kind. In the end they will drain and destroy, because they are alien to the kind of entity that you really are.

But we should be concerned, if we are interested (and if you're not, then why are you reading this book?), with three planes, or possibly even four. These are the higher positive-negative planes above our own existence.

The first is the plane that is reached after clinical death. The plane we enter after our departure from earth is rather like leaving an airport's international departure lounge. This is an astral plane of higher vibrations, but still material, which means that actually we still have a body, but slightly different to the one we had on earth. It is far more durable and has fewer aches and pains. To this next plane we take along our astral body, which is much, much lighter than our physical body but sometimes looks like our physical body. Just as a baby is joined to the mother at birth by an umbilical cord, so the physical body that we have for our chosen time is joined to the astral body by a similar cord, made up of psychic energy.

The reason that I'm sharing all this with you is that it is part of my life, the very foundation of my story, for it is the reality from which come all of my predictive abilities. I hope that by giving this information about the wider realities, the whole psychic world may be a little simpler to understand and, perhaps for some, not so frightening and complex.

Everyone has someone whom they love or are close to in the spirit world. That is why I was prompted to talk about this subject. Many people come to me, wanting help or knowledge about a friend, husband, wife, or loved one on the other side of this life. Reading this may help you to understand what life after death is like, in the secure knowledge that no ones dies for ever. Most people, ninety-nine per cent, are better off in the spirit world than they were on earth!

So let us return to our discussion about the astral cord. Once it is severed, then the spirit of the deceased person is able to ascend in joy and liberation to the next plane, where it will meet loved ones, close friends and teachers. It will be reunited in harmony with its enemies. On this plane directly above us, there is hardly any room for grudges or hate, although it is in many ways quite similar to our own life on earth. However, when people die in a clinical way, and the astral cord is not severed, then you get fascinating instances of people – and the documented cases are numerous – returning to earth with stories of the experience and feeling of death. The stupendous vision of the great and mystical tunnel of light with brilliance at the other end – then suddenly they are whipped back! Though their time was not appointed, they were fortunate enough to see the pathway to the spirit world.

For many people who are enlightened or aware, it is very easy to die well and pass into the spirit world without any problems at all. Sometimes it can be extremely difficult and traumatic because you are unaware that you are dead! I once had to convince a spirit that he was in fact dead, and he really needed a lot of proof! In the end he realized that he was dead, and left, happy that he was going to see his much loved wife, whom he hadn't seen for twenty long and lonely love-starved years.

Unfortunately, it happens from time to time that a spirit doesn't believe or can't understand it is dead. It becomes earthbound, wandering as a sad and bitter soul throughout the world in search of freedom, little realizing that it has the power to free itself from its misery.

Often, in my experience, a spirit doesn't want to leave the earth plane straight away, or is even frightened of death. Then it wants to go and see all its friends and say goodbye first. Eventually this causes a huge amount of problems. Some even don't realize where they are, and often psychics and mediums can help them far more than those in the spirit world. In the spirit world, they are, on the whole, far more concerned with what is going on there.

A good example of earthbound spirits being helped by mediums and psychics is the young pilots who died in the First and Second World Wars. Shot to pieces, burnt to death, the shock was far too much, and they had no idea at all that they were dead. Consequently they used to hang around airforce bases. The most famous in Britain is Biggin Hill, where it is literally choc-a-bloc of young ghostly pilots who are only too willing to ask you the time, have a chat, smoke a cigarette, or even ask to see a newspaper! Even the least psychic person around Biggin Hill will bump into one of these airmen, have a conversation, and then wonder, my God! why was he wearing a uniform that was forty years old!

Often earthbound spirits are here because something has been left undone. They can hang around for a day, a year, hundreds of years. One case that came to my attention was of a spirit that became earthbound out of revenge! Someone had poisoned him, and the dying man apparently knew who did it. He came back to get revenge. Far more frightening in reality than in a movie. Eventually the murderer confessed and went to prison!

The earthbound spirits, as are the spirits who are close to perfection, are not aware of time as we are in the earth plane. Once they understand that, they can be free from their torment; then they are ready to go forward to the next stage of their evolution. When we come into the earth plane we are all intended to suffer from a kind of psychic amnesia, which is for most of us essential if we are to make the most of our earthly life and the lessons that we have come here to learn.

But what happens to us when we get to the other side? Are we given a greetings telegram? A welcome speech from the Mayor? The key to the city? What happens? This is the sixty-four million pound question . . . I'll tell you.

When you get to the other side, to the spirit world, there is an initial period of adjustment, in order to get used to a new dimension of reality. It's rather like an astronaut returning from a mission in space; you are debriefed so you can adjust to new conditions again.

Then, as a spirit newly arrived in the spirit world, you begin to take your first few faltering steps towards enlightenment.

Often the spirit world can be an exact replica of how you lived your physical life. For example, if you were a heavy smoker, you will still think that you are smoking, and go through the astral equivalent! If you liked a particular hobby or sport, you will still pursue those activities! You will only stop once you realize that you no longer need the habits of your former life. There is then a period of living in that plane, the spirit world, where you learn new and exciting things, most important how to harmonize with that plane. You will also learn from mistakes made on earth through not harmonizing.

But the paramount lesson, and most probably the hardest for all of us, is how to love. Unconditionally. Without guarantees. To learn how to love creation and all that it contains. The ugly and the beautiful. It is also a time when we remove and transform hatred or tension, any bigotry or fear that we hold within us. Then we regain what we lost in our journey: our life, on the material earth plane.

The whole message is just variations of that. Everyone must be reincarnated several times before they go forward. There will come a time, I believe, that only so many chances to progress are given to us. If we have no chance to go forward, or even regress, we shall end in a static or contracted whirlpool of nothingness. Even, possibly, a black hole of non-consciousness.

We would be like this for ever and ever. We would cease to be. We would slowly lose our personal identities. I feel, unfortunately, that if history continues to be allowed to repeat itself along the highly negative and destructive pathways that it has followed in the past (remember we humans do not seem to learn from our mistakes), then this will happen to a great number of people. The consciousness of our future generations will be like starlight, lost in the cold depths of space.

Everyone on this earth now has lived before. There are no more new souls incarnating on to this earth plane. This destruction of consciousness is the nearest thing to the clumsy concept of the Final Judgement that is spoken about in the Bible and other great religious books. There are two states of hell. One is the negative-negative plane that we talked about before. The other, more subtle one is where there are spirit forms that tempt, acting as a force for evil. There *is* a definite force for evil. But most people are not spiritually advanced or perhaps psychic enough, fortunately, to experience it! Spirituality and being psychic do not always go together.

But let us not forget the force for good. Above the force for evil, and the force for good, above the material universes, there is an all-embracing neutral energy. Good and evil are the machines that drive the material universes. This neutral force is neither bad nor good. Call it God if you want. A name is useless to describe or confine it. I could say that it is everything and nothing, in every way and all ways. Or no way at all.

We are dealing now in paradox! But it seems to me

that paradox is the safety switch that takes control when logic short-circuits. We, humanity, make the good and the bad. We fuel energy into evil and good. Therefore we are able to create our own destiny by changing it.

After the plane of the spirit world, we will take on two further forms of 'body' and then matter will cease altogether. Then we shall become immersed in the energy of the spirit and, on a greater and much more exalted level, we shall become intelligence in its purest form.

We shall know that we exist. That will be enough. There will be no concept of the individual as on the earth or spirit world planes. We will, in this exalted plane, have no desire or appetites of any kind. Because we will be 'higher' and closer to the light of the universe, we will have greater joy. We shall know the difference between the reality of our existence on the earth plane and in the spirit world, and the transcendent reality of existence itself.

Humanity, and the individuals that comprise it, are all multi-layered – meaning there are many inner depths to our personality. Part of us is already in that highly exalted plane, as part of us could be on the lower planes. Often I use my awareness of these different planes to gain information for people with exceptional circumstances, who really do need a very special kind of help . . .

The higher the planes of existence go, the more beautiful life becomes. Although we are releasing ourselves from environmental influences as we progress from plane to plane, our human nature, or beingness, is retained. Therefore we desire beauty, and we receive it. But the beauty is beyond the beauty of the material world. Then there is the possibility of amnesia: we may forget entirely all that we ever did on the earth plane.

212

There are also those who exist on the higher planes and will never come to this earth plane. They are a higher form of life, an elevated form of spirit, whose concept of reality and the nature of life is as far beyond ours as ours is beyond the amoeba's.

Often these higher beings come in some form or another, usually unknown to us, to help humanity towards a better future. They also come for their own reasons. But that is very rare. They are, one could say, 'the eternal ones'.

They develop in various stages as well. The closest description one can use is angels. Not the angels of the Christians or other religions, but the prime movers of creation.

They are the ones who can get nearest to the light of the universe. We as spirit beings will reach our Utopia, which is bathed in the light of creation. But we will never reach that light itself.

Let us return to the spirit world, for it is the one dimension that we know the most about. It is very similar to the earth plane. There are houses there. Dwellings of some sort. Maybe they are built in the mind; it is quite possible. We are attracted, once we are there, for the large part of our duration, to those with whom we have the most in common.

From the spirit world we are extremely aware of our loved ones. We become concerned about the ways in which they live their lives on earth. Often those in the spirit world direct help towards their loved ones in order to make their earthly lives a little easier. At this point we are still very much influenced by a former life, so if our loved ones are distressed, sometimes souls will reincarnate out of urgency to help, or they can give messages through a medium. Often souls from the spirit world return to earth, because they become homesick!

There can be distortion in how messages from the spirit world are given or received by psychics or mediums. So the people from the spirit world are not always correct. They are not infallible. They need to be tested, because they live in another plane. Their sense of reality can be greatly removed from ours. Sometimes we reincarnate back on to earth because we are assigned to somebody, in order to be a major influence upon that person's life. This also happens in another way: we may be assigned to some person in order to be their spirit guide. A spirit guide, contrary to popular belief or opinion, does not follow one person throughout an entire lifetime. A spirit guide is only assigned to us to help us through particular stages in our life. No one, not even famous mediums or psychics, ever has a constant spirit guide with them. A spirit guide is somebody who has been through and experienced something similar to ourselves. In order to absolve a karma, without coming back to earth to do it, the spirit guide can actually steer you through the particular situation. Once it's done there's a psychic changing of the guard. Then another spirit guide may come to your help, if needed.

Many of the world's great artists have been inspired by glimpses of the spirit world through spirit guides directing them and giving them knowledge. If you listen to the music of Wagner you will find vivid descriptions of the spirit world. Also in the mythology of the Greeks, for example, one finds many references to the spirit world.

So in the spiritual reality I tune in to that which is already there. In other words, the destined pathways of my clients. There is never anything new to discover, only to be interpreted in new ways. That is why, for example, the writings of St John of the Cross are similar to Buddhist writings five hundred years before. They never knew anything about each other, but they were telling the same divine story. The life of Krishna is almost the same as the mythological writings about Jesus Christ. The same story is told, but different actors read the parts. The essential message behind all the different versions of this one story is: harmonize. Love and justice are the themes that run through them. They teach us to be only nothing more than ourselves; and yet, perhaps, that is the hardest thing to do. Not everyone on this earth or even in the higher planes is at the same stage of spiritual or material growth. So one only comes to understand the idea of harmony when one is ready and able to.

Therefore do not judge. It is better to be discreet and objective than judgemental or accusative. Justice waits around the corner for everyone. Live your life as best you can. That is the only true religion. People don't need to believe in orthodox religion at all. Some people may feel secure under that shadow, but the psychic and spiritual truth is that if you live in accordance with the moment, the moment will reveal the unity of life, the transcendence of spirit and freedom of the soul.

Enjoy life. Hurt no one. Love yourself as being part and parcel of a unique and ongoing eternity, and rejoice!

Sit down, if you can, for just a moment, and be still, and listen. Listen to yourself. Close your eyes. Relax, and you will hear, as I have over the last forty years, the spirit calling; forever and joyfully, the language of life.

Do everything in a way that will bring harmony to yourself and to others, in simple, ordinary and useful ways. Be practical in your pursuit of harmony. Do this so you can make a link with creation. Not neglecting the fact, the wonderful fact, of your own individuality! Do that, and it is the only prayer needed, because you are subscribing to the natural will of God, or whatever tag you like to place on the essence of life.

God is not an old man in the sky, as many people think, or a thinking, exacting god of justice. These ideas limit the indefinable to a space. The creation force is beyond space, or limits or definitions. There are adjudicators and guides that do dispense justice, but they are not the source. Why then, may we ask, has the misinterpretation of God grown up? Because of our knowledge of existence, the earth and the planets, and what the planets really are, and the whole mass of creation. We are just a pinprick, so we isolate and confine in order to understand the expression of that which can never be fully understood.

We had messages given to us by the eternal ones through prophets, whether modern or ancient. They say the same thing. Prophets such as Moses, Abraham and Jesus. To a much lesser extent Albert Schweitzer to the Africans he helped, Bob Marley to those who listened, Mohammed, Mahatma Gandhi, John Lennon, Mother Theresa. And there are countless thousands of unknown prophets: many a parson in his pulpit, or a rabbi in his synagogue, many a holy man, many a preacher. They are, as any human is, misguided in some way by their own dogmatic attitudes into thinking that one can limit the light of creation. In spite of their own shortcomings they can still bring great help and knowledge, often without understanding what they are doing.

If you want to be in harmony with nature you cannot achieve this through orthodox religion. But we must always remember mankind's great desire not to be alone, to identify with something greater that answers all the perplexing questions about life, to have a badge, to march behind the same banner. Common is the cry, 'We are the only ones who are right!' Whether a religious slogan or a football chant, it is all the same thing: mass hysteria. It is dangerous. It is limiting our progress towards higher development, and retarding the social and cultural growth of mankind.

Yet this need to belong, once organized, has done an awful lot of good. So if people want to come together, then let them do so in the knowledge that there is no dogma or set belief. We are here, perfect. Harmony just needs to be released from within each and every one of us.

In my opinion, the church of non-belief is the only church that could be accredited to 'God'. To have belief in something that *must* be there, namely God, is an insult.

Chapter 14

You Too Can Be a Prophet

Prophecy seldom profits the prophets. I have talked a lot about prediction and the importance of its role in my life, for it is my life. I have mentioned briefly prophecy and prophets, but I would like to go into the subject a little more. I've done prophecy on television, for magazines, in newspapers, but I have tried at all times to be very careful how I communicated what I think is going to take place. Prophecy is only any good if it helps to avoid catastrophes or gives insights into how to solve serious problems for once and for all.

First of all, I've often been quoted in the media as saying, that 'every man is somebody's Buddha'. But I feel that the phrase should be changed in today's climate of sexual equality to 'every person is somebody's Buddha'. I mean this in the sense of teacher. A prophet, in my opinion, could be anyone from Jesus of Nazareth to Harry Crystals, the lavatory keeper at the gents' public toilets in Leicester Square!

We all can be at certain times prophets, because we all have the bright spark of divinity blazing within us, and that is the only qualification needed to spread the words of an inspired prophecy. Prophecy isn't always about world events and huge tidal waves, or an invasion of earth by men from Mars, or that the end of the world will be the twenty-second of yesterday. That is not what prophecy is about. Most of the time, ordinary people prophesy without realizing it. To be a prophet, then, is to relate information, or to speak of that which is to come. Therefore every genuine and responsible psychic is a prophet in varying degrees. Most people are prophets at some time, because of the natural sixth sense, or extra-sensory perception, that is running through our psychic make-up. It is the nature of human beings to be psychic.

However, tradition and orthodoxy would have us believe a prophet is someone special who is inspired by God or a cause, and with a bolt of invisible lightning will reveal the truth for all mankind. Cobblers to that! A prophet is someone who leads us to better under-standing of our everyday life. For example, a bank manager is a prophet, when he tells us about our over-draft and what's going to happen if it's not fixed! How many of you have had that prophecy? It usually puts the fear of God into you, doesn't it? But the job of true prophecy is to help us to learn why we are on earth.

Any prophecies that lead us in those directions are genuine. Remember, they don't have to be about huge and dramatic things. They may be concerned with the small things of life, for the small things of life, the everyday routines, are often the things by which we learn important values such as discipline, patience, and so on. Since human beings are not perfect, we have to learn the same lessons many times over.

The prophets who have made it into the pages of history books have become the heroes and heroines of mystery. Someone along the line has done an excellent public relations job on their image with high-quality advertising. Perhaps a hundred years from now, Bob Geldof will go down in the history books as a prophet of compassion who, taking his flaming bush, the media and the recording industry, helped to save the starving millions in the barren lands of Africa.

Where would Jesus have been without St Paul? In reality, Jesus is probably turning in his grave under the ruins of the old fortress Masada, highly annoyed at what St Paul has done. Jesus wasn't a Christian! The prophet who sounded his own trumpet most was Mohammed. But in all the great religious books of the prophets, there is a great deal of wisdom to be learned. Whether they said what has been attributed to them or not is totally irrelevant, because the person who did write those words, in order to promote the party line, wrote wisdom. And that is all that matters.

One only has to look at the prophecies of Nostradamus. All his prophecies are of warning, and there you find instructions given to the world at large to watch out in case we all wipe ourselves off the face of the earth.

It doesn't necessarily follow that for a person to be a prophet he has to be good. He may drink too much. Have a different sexual partner every night. Take drugs. Eat meat. Tell lies. Steal from tourists. Whatever. But then again a person who is a prophet may be the total reverse of all those things. After death, great prophets always used to be given fancy titles, and of course were credited with things they never said. Often prophecy is politics. The two seem to go hand in hand. For example, Jesus of Nazareth was voted God by six to seven at the first Christian Council. Jesus was just a Jewish politician who had the good sense to capitalize on the messiah story that the population believed in at the time. He was a real king trying to reclaim his kingdom from the Romans.

Another great prophet-politician was Moses. He was called the law-giver. Did God give him the laws of the

Ten Commandments? Who knows? It was a very good way of uniting a divided tribe, giving them a sense of unity and security.

Prophecy is real. It is a definite force that has helped to mould many of the world's greatest cultures and runs through every mythology. My own life and the work I do is a living example of this. I do an act of prophecy ten times a day sometimes. But every prophecy that I do for a client also affects the world.

I have numerous letters praising not me but the psychic abilities that come through me. I have constant telephone calls just to thank me – so many that now I have to have a separate line especially to handle this wonderful deluge of warmth and appreciation. I have many people saying to me, 'Mr Lee, I don't know how you did it, but what you said happened to me exactly in the way you said it would!'

Often I am so busy that I don't understand the exact complexity of what I am saying to a client. But the most important thing is that my client does. The reason why my clients understand, even if I do not, is that I am speaking directly to their souls. Their souls have ears, so to speak, and the vibrant realities of what the higher forces say through me awaken the client's sleeping soul, and since knowledge liberates, often my clients leave me feeling as if a warm fire is ablaze in their hearts. They walk out into the world more aware and far less insensitive, knowing that they can change their destiny if they so desire.

Mozart wrote a symphony at seven; that act of artistic creation was an act of prophecy. I couldn't play, let alone write, a symphony at ninety-seven, but I know the scales of music. In a different way from Wolfgang, I understand the psychic harmony, and thus I make my own music, which as you know comes from the higher realms.

We all have the psyche within us, the inbuilt oracle, and we can look back with the deep scrutiny of psychic awareness. The reason why we can look forward, or look back towards the past, is because time itself is a great illusion.

We make time a reality, in the sense that we live our lives to a set routine, or work to a deadline, or create values based on time. Time is an invention of man by which to measure his existence, but it has become so much a part of everyone's make-up on this planet that people have become controlled by it. We let time trap us into living often less than satisfactory lives, and by prophecy we can discover that our lives need not be restricted by time and routines, but can be greatly nourished, improved and made fun by delving deeply into the limitless potential of the human spirit.

You can be a prophet to yourself. The whole aim of being psychic is to discover self-knowledge, and then apply it honestly to the improvement of your circumstances.

The world is fast entering into a new age, and this age is the age of doubt, and yet the age of certainty, for as more and more people doubt the validity of the way in which they live their lives, and the way the world is going, they turn towards the certainty of inner knowledge. But many get confused along the way, so it is important to think: is my inner understanding realistic? Is it practical? Will help me to live in the world, and be with it, but not controlled by it?

Prophecy is really a very misunderstood subject. Now in these final years of the twentieth century, it seems that the psychic and paranormal are starting to become universally accepted as being aspects of the human personality. In time, everyone will have psychic and prophetic powers in abundance. Perhaps we are heading towards a psychic technological future, where mankind's psychic abilities will be integrated with our technical and scientific progress. The new frontiers of reality discovered by science have been known by psychics since man first walked the earth.

And so, as a psychic, I welcome a bright new future where the psychic and the sciences work hand in hand in the exploration of the material universe and the endless potential of the human mind.

Chapter 15

Where There is Faith, Even the Tooth of a Dog Will Emit Light

You may wonder why I started the final chapter of this part of my story with such a strange title. It is an old Tibetan saying, which means that if we have faith in something – whether an idea, an object or even a person – and we concentrate all of our faith upon this one thing, we can by the power of our faith make it holy, because we are holy. Therefore because we are holy we can choose as we like the way in which we want to live our lives, according to how we, consciously or not, interpret the light of creation. We shouldn't judge others, but we can give opinions. Even as a psychic my predictions are only opinions that have come true. They are not judgements, for a judgement implies no mercy, and mercy is mankind's only redeeming feature.

To explain the idea further I'll tell you the story of how the saying came into being, because whether it is true or not, the idea is true and that is all that matters. If you've never been to Tibet, that country of psychic secrets, now here is your chance! You don't even have to leave your chair!

Once upon a time, there was a very old woman, all wrinkly, who suffered terribly from rheumatism. She lived, much to her satisfaction and joy, on the magical borders of the holy land. This old lady also had a son, who was very happy that he, too, lived with his mother on the borders of the holy land, because the son was a bit of a social climber, and as everyone knew, to live on the borders of the holy land was awfully chic and a real status symbol.

Now once a year the son had to go on business to Tibet by caravan, and every year before the son set off, the old lady would say to her son, 'Son, please bring back with you a relic of some truly saintly holy man.' The son would promise faithfully to do so, but he'd always forget because his mind was on other things in the big city. Fast women, gambling and, of course, business.

When he got home his mother asked him for the relic of the holy man, and the boy was upset, because he was as thick as two planks of wood. Next year came along, and again his mother asked him to get a relic of a holy man. She begged him not to forget, for it would make her so happy! He wrote a note in his diary so that this time he would get a relic of a holy man for his dear old mother. Once and for all.

He went off to do his trading, and on his way back as the caravan was travelling up the road towards the mountain pass that spelt home, the boy remembered his mother's wish. He was upset. He didn't want to face his mother without anything, and on the side of the road he saw the bleached skull of a dog, and he ripped a tooth with a mighty tug from its jaw, thinking that this would do – his mother would never know the difference.

As he approached the entrance to his mother's house, he said to his mother, 'At last I have brought you back the thing that your heart most desired. The tooth is a relic of a holy man. Are you happy, Mother?' She was

225

indeed. She did a geriatric skip and hop, and with great reverence placed the relic in a special place in her home, adoring it and praying to it at all hours of the day and night.

Quickly the local newspaper got hold of the story and published a sensational account and, of course, rumours and gossip, and even legends, began to grow up around this holy tooth. Breakfast cereal manufacturers wanted to use it in their advertising. People for miles around, even from other countries, came to worship this tooth. Mothers would come praying fervently that their children would have cavity-free teeth, and so no dental bills! Then, after a couple of years had passed, with all these people offering their worship, the tooth began to give off a dazzling brilliant white-and-blue light, there was the sound of a heavenly choir, and a shining golden aura began to form around the tooth. What had happened? Everyone wanted to know! Even some of the cynics were converted. All the devout worship of the faithful through the concentration of their faith had made the tooth holy, but, of course, the holiness came from within the spirits of the faithful.

This is the reason why all over the world holy relics have psychic or supernatural effects upon people, and on a larger and more important scale, it is why concentrated hope, or faith, can change the world from a path of chaos, confusion and possible destruction, into an avenue of peace, harmony and cooperation. The planet Earth has a bright future to it. All we should realize is that the future is in our hands, now.

In this, the first part of my life story, I have only been able to include a small portion of all that has happened to me. There are many people who are not included, places I have seen, strange experiences involving my psychic abilities. Yet I realize that I have so much more to do, to express. Everything must take a step, even if it is a small one, towards the Light. Every step we take is the step that we're meant to make. I often, especially in my earlier life, rebelled against having such strong psychic powers, mainly at times when I was impatient with the world and didn't fully understand what my role in life was to be.

The last years of the twentieth century are going to see a psychic revolution in the world. Many more thousands of people will respond to their own spirits' call, and take the first few faltering steps towards the experience of a higher, deeper, exhilarating reality. The psychic experience of life. Even now, more people are taking an interest in the development of their psychic powers; they are starting to accept that there is life after death.

When people understand the causes of their problems, they are on the whole able to remove the problem and the cause, and as we enter the last part of this century it occurs to me, especially through all the readings that I have done over the years, that this is the century in which the earth and its people have suffered more global traumas than at any other time in time history. Why?

What causes and effects are we as a race, or the planet as a living being, trying to work out? Have we got only so long before we all witness the next stage in the evolution of man? Just as we evolved from cavemen, to farmers, to city dwellers, to builders of nations, constructors of empires, inventors of technology, perhaps the next stage concerns the development of the psychic faculties of our much underestimated minds and brains.

Perhaps the year two thousand will see the infant stage of mental and psychic forces interacting with science and technology. Who knows where, for example, in the frontiers of space development and exploration, the psychic abilities of man might be put to good use?

More than ever mankind is in search of insight into the problems of living in the twentieth century. So if in the search for meaning the psychic is used as the vehicle of understanding, well and good, but also use reason, restraint and intelligence. To try to make a religion out of the psychic, as many have done in the past, is a fatal mistake which leads to trouble. Mankind has a great ability for hysteria, and for directing its hysteria into forms or ideas that seem to be common sense. It is easy for a group of people to justify their hysteria if they believe that it will bring them salvation. The psychic world does not bring salvation, nothing can. The very idea of salvation is a con, for in the law of the universe everyone is his own saviour.

People cling to the psychic world as if it were the answer to all their problems. That is not a healthy attitude to have! It is far more important to live for the moment in the moment. The title of my book is *The Spirit Calls* because the spirit within all of us, that energy which is beyond death or time, calls us in its own silent language to go forward, not to stop and dream in the memories past, or to cling to things in order to hide our fears. No, the spirit within each of us encourages us to be brave and have courage and to express joy in our everyday lives. No one ever has a trouble-free life, because if they did they would not be here on earth, or in the spirit world, but in the dizzy heights of the higher realms of pure intelligence. So when you have troubles it is best to stay calm, still, and let the spirit call you into action, and you will be guided into the right path of action.

Once guided into the right action, trust your higher self always, and you will find that as you go about your daily business, you will create a little heaven of your very own on earth.

Then you will find that peace of mind is the greatest treasure that any man or woman could have. Peace of mind is the only legacy that we can leave to the next generation. In all my years as a psychic it is the one thing that people have most wanted to find; some people – in fact, many people – have come to me, thinking that I could give it to them. I was always saddened at having to tell them that this was not the case. Each of us must search for it individually, for no one person's peace is the same as another's.

But of course my predictions often help to point my clients in the right direction. The path to peace has no signposts or rest-rooms or roadside cafés on the way, and often when we are looking for it we have to take one step back before we go forwards, or fall down flat on our faces before we look straight up and into its light.

Thinking back to my childhood, especially because of the book, prompted me to return to my childhood haunts. The house I loved so much in Malden Place is now gone, only a ghost in the memory of the neighbourhood. A modern block of executive luxury flats now stands towering on the site that served as a haven of safety during the last days of the war for my family, friends and neighbours. As you know, I was a baby then, but I can still remember the faces of those men and women who tried to make me smile with their songs and the strident tones of a single ukelele. I wondered if the bomb shelter was still there. I sensed that it had given up the ghost as it was now blocked up.

I stood there feeling the sensations of the past. There was no corner shop with the tall Mr Richards and his pails as he went on the morning milk round. There was no more children's chatter as they played together on the street. The neighbourhood that I knew had now gone, faded away. It was full of fast-moving youths and their girlfriends in exotic cars, out enjoying life, as they should, to the full.

Many of the faces that I knew in my childhood have most probably passed on into the spirit world. They would be laughing still, friends united again on the other side. My mother would be free there – free from hallucinations and strokes. My father would be there, ruminating in his own quiet way.

Little did I know then, in the innocent years of my childhood, that I would one day be working for the service of higher forces. I wanted to be a traveller, when a child, not a fireman, or an engine-driver, or even a policeman. I wanted to travel the world, to see strange sights and strange people, to go, as most little boys wanted, exploring tropical jungles. Strangely enough, I have done a lot of such travelling and I have also travelled where few ever go in this life. Many are called, but few find the way.

I found the way to the psychic because it was my destiny. My childhood was a happy, exciting time, but as I began to realize that I was different from other children, my gifts began to worry me. Often I would become depressed because I could see things that even my best friends couldn't. Even Bernard, my closest friend, wasn't able to see the spirit people I saw. It took me a long time to accept the fact that not everyone had the gift as much as I.

One memory that will always stay with me is when, at the funeral of my mother in a beautiful church, Bernard and the whole Nolan family turned up to give us their condolences. As my mother was buried, I felt the eternity of the spirit, and the air around me began to fill with a gentle warmth, a happiness and a sigh of relief. I felt my mother's load go from her shoulders, and I knew that she was smiling.

The afternoon air was still but from out of nowhere there came a gentle breeze, a spirit breeze. It was one last gentle touch from my mother before she finally departed this earth. I looked up and saw Bernard giving me a reassuring smile, for in that moment he had sensed something of the eternal.

I have always questioned everything I do, even when prompted by Spirit. The more I question, the stronger are the replies. If you ask, you will always get an answer, but remember the answer may not come in the form you expect, and it may not come immediately. It may come weeks, months or even years later.

Time, like the past, is a curtain which can be parted. Whenever we go over the past, it is the spirit world's way of prompting us to take stock of our actions.

As I grow older I realize how very valuable every moment is, how every second of my life, how every beat of my heart, how every blink of my eyes takes up time, takes up space. This reminds me of my mortality.

Life is a game. It seems long, but is in fact incredibly short. It is the only game where the rules change from moment to moment. But instead of chopping and changing rules, why not throw them away altogether, and discover the real rules – those that your spirit engraved upon your heart.

I have found that although I question, the only rules, the only true morality is the morality that is within me.

The one I brought with me to earth from the spirit world.

We all bring our own morality with us from the spirit world. But, as I said earlier, we often come here in a state of forgetting the knowledge and wonder of the spirit world, where life seemed like a dream. Many philosophers, mystics, and psychics have said that the world is like a dream, because the reality of the spirit world is so close that they have glimpsed the higher worlds – in a sense died and been reborn to the nature of reality.

Reality is like a heatwave, or a snowflake just before it touches a window pane, dissolving into another form, taking on a new existence. Reality isn't static; it changes, fluxes, forms into strange shapes and reforms again. Our life is not the substance of reality, but the imprint that we make upon it, just as the rain drops into a pond and causes rings in the water, or the wind blows the leaves in the trees or forms the waves into shape.

I have made a resolution to let the past make me wise, the future make me confident, and for the present to be at peace. The only thing that anyone can do in life is to become. This is not a riddle, for becoming is more essential than being.

I look forward to the time when I can share with you again glimpses, shadows and highlights from my life. This is not the time to say goodbye, but bon voyage.

PS I was once told that age is a bad travelling companion. But if you travel in harmony with your spirit through life, age will be nothing but a way of measuring your years on earth, and all that you have yet to learn!

THE BEGINNING

THE BOOK OF CHINESE BELIEFS

Frena Bloomfield

Earth magic, ghost weddings, passports to the after-life: the spirit world of the Chinese exists side-by-side with everyday reality, and affects every aspect of Chinese life from diet and decor to getting married or opening a business.

Frena Bloomfield has lived and worked in Hong Kong and has talked in depth to many practitioners of the magic arts. *The Book of Chinese Beliefs* is a fascinating introduction to a rich culture where the dead are ever-present and even the siting of a house or village is governed by the laws of earth magic.

YOUR PSYCHIC WORLD A-Z
An everyday guide

Ann Petrie

Everyone is psychic.

Everyone has the ability to develop extrasensory perception, but few know what to do with it.

Taking examples from everyday life, this book looks at the efficiency of your energy and your love, and presents a whole new perspective on the psychic world.

It explains *why* certain unusual or uncanny situations occur, and how to handle them in ways most beneficial to you and those around you.

This guide tells you what to do if you — Meet a ghost, a ghoul or a poltergeist; Feel you've been cursed; Fall in love at first sight; Remember places you know you've never been to before; Have dreams that come true; Need to protect yourself from psychic attack — plus many more pieces of essential advice on relating to the psychic world around you.

Ann Petrie is a psychic-astrologer who combines her gifts in a unique way in writing, broadcasting and counselling.

THE HANDBOOK OF CHINESE HOROSCOPES

Theodora Lau

Are you a sentimental but crafty Rat, a serious and dutiful Ox, or a captivating but unpredictable Tiger? Here, in the most comprehensive book ever written on Chinese astrology, you can find out which of the twelve animal signs of the lunar calendar is yours, how your sign is affected by the Yin and Yang, how your Moon sign and your Sun sign affect each other – and which of the other animal signs you're compatible with.

BESTSELLING NON-FICTION FROM ARROW

All these books are available from your bookshop or news-agent or you can order them direct. Just tick the titles you want and complete the form below.

☐	THE GREAT ESCAPE	Paul Brickhill	£1.75
☐	A RUMOR OF WAR	Philip Caputo	£2.50
☐	A LITTLE ZIT ON THE SIDE	Jasper Carrott	£1.50
☐	THE ART OF COARSE ACTING	Michael Green	£1.50
☐	THE UNLUCKIEST MAN IN THE WORLD	Mike Harding	£1.75
☐	DIARY OF A SOMEBODY	Christopher Matthew	£1.25
☐	TALES FROM A LONG ROOM	Peter Tinniswood	£1.75
☐	LOVE WITHOUT FEAR	Eustace Chesser	£1.95
☐	NO CHANGE	Wendy Cooper	£1.95
☐	MEN IN LOVE	Nancy Friday	£2.75

Postage ......

Total ......

ARROW BOOKS, BOOKSERVICE BY POST, PO BOX 29, DOUGLAS, ISLE OF MAN, BRITISH ISLES

Please enclose a cheque or postal order made out to Arrow Books Ltd for the amount due including 15p per book for postage and packing both for orders within the UK and for overseas orders.

Please print clearly

NAME ....

ADDRESS ....

....

Whilst every effort is made to keep prices down and to keep popular books in print, Arrow Books cannot guarantee that prices will be the same as those advertised here or that the books will be available.

BESTSELLING FICTION FROM ARROW

All these books are available from your bookshop or news-agent or you can order them direct. Just tick the titles you want and complete the form below.

☐	THE COMPANY OF SAINTS	Evelyn Anthony	£1.95
☐	HESTER DARK	Emma Blair	£1.95
☐	1985	Anthony Burgess	£1.75
☐	2001: A SPACE ODYSSEY	Arthur C. Clarke	£1.75
☐	NILE	Laurie Devine	£2.75
☐	THE BILLION DOLLAR KILLING	Paul Erdman	£1.75
☐	THE YEAR OF THE FRENCH	Thomas Flanagan	£2.50
☐	LISA LOGAN	Marie Joseph	£1.95
☐	SCORPION	Andrew Kaplan	£2.50
☐	SUCCESS TO THE BRAVE	Alexander Kent	£1.95
☐	STRUMPET CITY	James Plunkett	£2.95
☐	FAMILY CHORUS	Claire Rayner	£2.50
☐	BADGE OF GLORY	Douglas Reeman	£1.95
☐	THE KILLING DOLL	Ruth Rendell	£1.95
☐	SCENT OF FEAR	Margaret Yorke	£1.75

Postage _____

Total _____